A Gift of God

A Gift of God
My Path to Priesthood

DAVID M. CHAMBERLAIN

INSPIRING WORDS PRESS
HIGHLANDS, NC

ISBN 978-0-692-35876-4
Printed in the United States of America
First Printing, 2016

Designed by Lynn Willoughby
Cover illustration by Christopher K. Baxter

Inspiring Words Press
120 Sky Water Lane
Highlands, NC 28741
www.lynnwilloughby.com

Dedicated to the one true living God—Father, Son, and Holy Spirit—in thanksgiving for the family with whom I have been so lovingly blessed.

Acknowledgments

Based primarily on the journal I kept during my preparation for the ministry, I began this book in 1973 as a way of commemorating the three wonderful years that I spent at the Virginia Theological Seminary from 1968–1971. Soon the demands of parish ministry caused me to put it away until a more opportune time presented itself. I worked on it some during my sabbatical leave in 1995, but it was not until retirement that I completed my work—and then only because of the commitment of other people.

First and foremost, I want to thank my wife Patty who literally wrote this book for me, serving as my scribe, typing on a computer while I dictated from my notes. Without her labor of love, this work would never have been finished. Also thanks are due our son Michael and daughter Carolyn, who offered technical and emotional support, and also those friends and parishioners who read parts of the manuscript in its developmental stages and offered revision and refinement along the way.

Next, author Lynn Willoughby agreed to serve as my editor and publisher. I am most indebted to her and to Christopher Baxter, who drew the artwork for the cover and chapter subdivisions.

I certainly want to thank, as well, all the people whose lives touched mine at VTS. Those experiences became the essence of this narrative.

Lastly, I want to thank all of those at the Virginia Theological Seminary who provided me with journal articles, newspaper columns, information sheets, and handouts— all of which helped me to reconstruct the events that are recorded in the text. I have tried to give them proper credit in the body of this work.

DMC

*For by grace you have been saved through faith; and
this is not your own doing, it is the gift of God. . . .*
Ephesians 2:8

THE JUNIOR YEAR

CHAPTER 1

The scenery along interstate highways can be monotonous after a while, but the drive from Roanoke to Front Royal along I-81, which cuts right through the heart of the Shenandoah Valley, escapes that problem by following the highs and lows of the beautiful Blue Ridge Mountains. It was on that road where David Morrow Chamberlain found himself one day, leaving his home to begin a new life in the ministry.

After traveling from Chattanooga along the back roads and through the stop-and-go towns of eastern Tennessee up to Bristol, it was not surprising to feel even his new Volkswagen Beetle come alive as it freely opened up to the higher speeds of interstate travel. But alive and free were the last things that David was feeling on that particular Thursday morning in September 1968.

In fact, ever since he had awakened in Roanoke at the Holiday Inn that morning, the twenty-one-year-old had felt as if he were in some sort of a daze, not really wanting to make the trip, but feeling compelled to do so like some sort of unfeeling robot, programmed to run in a certain direction or respond in a particular fashion.

The young man really felt as if he were numbly void of life, it having ended the night before as far as he was concerned. For everything that he had ever known or loved was in the past, back in Chattanooga, Tennessee. And there he was in Virginia. Steve McQueen's last line from the motion picture *The Sand Pebbles* kept running through his mind: "What the hell happened?"

What had happened was that David Morrow Chamberlain, recent graduate of the University of Chattanooga and former Big Man on Campus, was on his way to a seat of higher learning—a theological seminary to be exact. And just exactly what he would encounter, he had absolutely no idea.

"Preparation for the ministry, the Episcopal priesthood? God help me," he thought to himself. "What in the world am I doing?"

Oh sure, the up-and-coming divinity student had talked to the bishop of his diocese about advanced religious education, and even been assured by the prelate that if the Holy Spirit wanted him, He'd get him. And the English major had gone through all of the red tape necessary in order to become a postulant for Holy Orders. But that had just seemed like something to do back during the comfortable routine of college life, a justifiable way of making some plans for what he thought he *might* like to *consider* doing for a vocation. At that time, his decision hadn't involved any sacrifice. Now he was really putting it on the line.

Then other fears began to slither in. What if he didn't like it? What would he do then? Would he have to carry the Bible and a Book of Common Prayer around all day? Would they lock him up at night? How much would he have to pray? Would he have to go to church all the time?

"Damn!" David exclaimed silently. "This must be what a soldier feels like going off to war, prepared to offer himself for a glorious cause." At the least, the Tennessean wondered if a soldier could possibly feel any worse.

As the Bee Gees' "I've Gotta Get a Message to You" played

on the radio, a car slipped past the new, green Beetle, which David's father had given to him as a college graduation present. The Ford Mustang was full of girls, all four of whom were fairly attractive and friendly enough to wave. David waved back, of course, and smiled, wishing that an opportunity might present itself to do more.

"Girls," he mused. "Maybe Virginia has some girls. Maybe I won't have to be celibate. Maybe Patty and I will even get married one day. Dear Lord, what the hell happened?"

The most recent acquirer of a German car hardly even remembered turning off of I-81 onto State Highway 55. At the time, that was the most direct way to Interstate 66, or what had been constructed of it to date. I-66 got you to Washington by connecting to the beltway that circled the District of Columbia. Interstate 95 spooled off of that beltway, and the exit to the Virginia Theological Seminary in Alexandria rolled off of I-95.

But David misread a sign, got off of the beltway too early, and wound up rambling around northern Virginia for over an hour. Finally though, he stopped at a gas station to ask for directions and discovered that he was only about two blocks from his destination.

Upon being informed that he was not hopelessly lost nor too far from his goal, the school's new enrollee began to feel his stomach tighten as he released his last grip on the possibility of turning back, going home, or waking up to find the whole thing to be just a dream. The knot in his stomach was comparable to the feeling of having been told he'd just flunked a final exam. But, back into his vehicle he got, and up the road he drove.

While looking for road signs, David suddenly spotted a tower of some sort and decided to head for it. Sure enough, he soon came to the intersection of Quaker Lane and Seminary

Road. Not too far away was the wall surrounding the campus, and the tower he had spotted was rising from the top of a red brick building. As the Tennessean approached the gates, the lettering loomed large: "The Protestant Episcopal Theological Seminary in Virginia." David turned into the driveway and slowly ascended the hill.

His whole life seemed to flash in front of him—from his earliest childhood recollections to the tender kiss of the previous night when he had put Patty on the bus. Patty, his childhood sweetheart, was venturesome and loving enough to have ridden all the way to Roanoke so that he would not be by himself for the first part of this new chapter in his life, only to spend the entire night herself, riding an uncomfortable bus back to Chattanooga. Ah, Patty! Oh, how he wished she were with him.

Thoughts of the previous day ran through David's mind—the trip itself, the film *With Six You Get Eggroll* at the Jefferson Theater, dinner at the Holiday Inn talking with Patty about their future over Whiskey Sours, and then . . . goodbye.

"No, not goodbye," he said as he held her close, "just so long."

His father had taught him that. As a Christian, you never have to say goodbye.

David had watched the bus leave the station. After a brief prayer for Patty's well being, he had ridden back to the motel—alone, as was she. After watching a little of *The Tonight Show* with Johnny Carson, he cut the lights off and stared at the dark ceiling. He tried to pray for himself but felt that life as he knew it was over. And that seemed to be all he could think about. Thus his prayer was a brief one.

He used the same prayer the next afternoon as "Sam," the Volkswagen affectionately named for an old friend, chugged up the seminary drive—the same prayer that Christ uttered in His last words from the Cross: "Father, into Thy hands I commit my spirit!"

John Harrison McCann was sitting alone in his room in Wilmer Hall. The sign on the door read "# 204," and right beneath the number was a name plate holder for a calling card. Filling that slot was about all that he had managed to accomplish since arriving on the seminary grounds at 2:00 that afternoon. That was almost three hours ago, and he was becoming slightly frustrated that he had yet to get off of his hind quarters to begin the process of "creating" his room.

Some room! Both the walls and the ceiling were off-white in color. The white chest of drawers was built into the white wall next to the white door on one side and the white sink on the other. The sink stood next to a white closet. The only color in the whole room, if you could call it that, was the dull gray of the bed mattress, a brown desk, a black lamp, a green wastebasket, and a duller green seat in the gray metal chair on which he was sitting. That was it except for the black alternating squares in the otherwise white linoleum floor. That room was a lot different from the old one at home in St. Joseph, Missouri or even his dorm room at the University of Kansas, where he had lived until his graduation in 1967 with a degree in English.

John had been a dorm counselor during one of those four college years and then had stayed on for the 1967–68 academic year as an assistant instructor in English. But that was all in the past. Presently, he was in the middle of a new world, a world wherein he would dwell for the majority of the next thirty-three months.

Though his new abode was not exactly a suite, there were some advantages. The way in which the chest of drawers was built into the wall did allow for more room and floor space, and it was nice to have an individual sink and medicine cabinet so that roommates weren't crawling over each other in the morning trying to shave.

And the view wasn't bad. Room #204 faced east looking out across the seminary quadrangle. And it was at that window that the chunky man from Missouri with a full shock of black hair had sat staring for almost two hours. Though somewhat irritated at not having accomplished more, John could easily rationalize his rest period, for it had been a full and long two-day drive. And besides being physically exhausted, he was also emotionally drained. He had no idea what he was getting himself into.

"That was the longest drive I've ever made in my life," John thought to himself, "and in so many more ways than miles."

Upon John's arrival, he had been greeted by a young man whom the Missourian hoped might turn out to be a dorm mate, but whom, after informing him of the location of his room, wound up heading in the opposite direction. Other than that one lone soul, John had yet to meet anyone else other than Ted Boswell. Ted was a six-foot "middler," or second year student, who hailed from the Diocese of Arkansas and who had arrived on the campus early because he was the dorm proctor.

McCann felt an immediate kinship, fondly remembering the year he himself had served as counselor of his dorm at KU. Ted had helped him in with his bags, greeted him probably as warmly as anyone can greet a total stranger in a new environment, and promptly departed for a meeting. So, having set down his bags and claimed his room with his personal card on the door, John had taken a quick look at his surroundings, then pulled a chair up to the open window and straddled it with his 5 feet 11 1/2 inch, one hundred and seventy pound frame.

Off in the distance, he heard a marching band, reminding him of his days of playing the clarinet back at his university. But before his mind followed that train of memories farther into the past, he spied a shiny green VW on the other side of the quadrangle.

The Beetle was exactly like his, save for the color. John's was sky blue. Perhaps the green one was newer; he couldn't quite tell. But anyway the car had stopped, and the driver had gotten out, most likely to ask for directions from the two men standing in front of the main building of the academic complex. John thought he detected one of the fellows pointing right at him. He was confirmed in his belief that another resident of the dorm was about to arrive on the scene when the VW chugged off around the quadrangle to halt right in front of Wilmer Hall.

Feeling that a relationship might have a better chance of getting off the ground if he initiated a greeting, John got up and hastened out of his room toward the steps. As he came into the downstairs area, his eyes caught sight of several bags that had been pushed into open doorways, but there were no signs of people around.

"Boy, I must have really been in a trance not to have heard those folks come in," he thought to himself, figuring future dorm mates must have arrived, deposited their gear, surveyed their surroundings, and taken off for parts unknown while they still had the opportunity.

Speeding on down the corridor, John almost ran into the

dorm proctor, who had just come back from his meeting. He chatted with Ted impatiently, trying his best to get around him and out the door. It was not that he disliked this Boswell fellow at all. It was just that the second-year student was already in the groove with twelve months behind him and friends already made. The man from Missouri simply wanted a chance to interact with someone on the same launching pad as himself.

Too late! As Ted rambled on about John-didn't-even-know-what, the door opened. In walked a young man who appeared to be in his early twenties wearing green shorts and a plaid shirt, it's tail hanging out. He had short brown hair, was fairly nice looking, and soon proved to have a resonant speaking voice laced with a charming Tennessee accent.

David nodded, said hello to the two, and introduced himself. Boswell started to respond, but John cut him off by extending his hand to claim the new associate as his own. With a toothy grin and a firm handshake, John introduced himself then backed off a little so the other member of the trio could offer a greeting.

A few words along the lines of "I'm from so-and-so" and "just got in" followed, then Ted excused himself to go assist in the kitchen, announcing that supper was imminent.

"Gosh, it is 5:00 already, isn't it?" said the man from Tennessee, thus beginning a short discourse on his wanderings through northern Virginia.

John responded that fortunately he had experienced no difficulty on the road, and in fact had driven right to the gate. He had gotten there almost too early, since hardly anyone else seemed to be around at the time.

"Well, that's a great way to be welcomed to your new home!" David quipped, and John knew that he had found a friend.

"Unpacked yet?" the Tennessean asked.

"No," replied the Missourian, "but everything's in my room. Which one are you in?"

"Number 104."

"That's right below me!" John said. "Can I help you move in?"

"How could I refuse such a generous and gracious offer?" David replied. They strolled out of Wilmer Hall to the laden car.

The two talked about the coincidence of their each having a Volkswagen but agreed that it was not all that unusual since, as far as they were concerned, VW made the best car on the road. While they discussed the attributes and qualities of German automobile manufacturing, the two new dorm residents began to unload the vehicle.

John departed with the first set of luggage, but before David could follow he felt that he just had to sit down on the front seat for a minute, thank God for a safe journey, and then whisper to himself with a sigh, "Well, here I am."

But knowing that if he lingered too long it might result in melancholy, the latest student to arrive on the seminary scene got up, picked up an armload of clothes, and moved toward his room, passing his new acquaintance in the hallway on the way back for more items.

John reached into the back of the car to get a plaid shoe bag brimming with books. But when he yanked it, he found himself holding on to just the handle.

"Great," he thought. "A fine way to start a friendship—with destruction of property."

Desperately trying to figure out how he could salvage either the bag or the bond, John could think of no alternative other than to confess his crime upon David's return.

"Don't worry about it," his colleague replied. "That thing is older than God anyway."

John sighed in relief.

Having finally gotten everything unpacked and their cars parked behind the dorm, the two new comrades decided that they had better begin to get their rooms in order, having about half an hour before dinner at 6:00. John went upstairs, and David slowly crossed the threshold of what would be his home for almost three years.

"It's as empty as I feel," he thought to himself.

And not having even the energy to put his calling card in the name plate holder on the door as his companion had done, David sat down on the bed and stared at his bags. Out of the corner of his eye, he spotted an envelope on the floor that had drifted aside by the windward draft of the door opening. He stood almost mechanically, picked it up, opened it, and read:

> Mr. David M. Chamberlain
> c/o The Virginia Seminary
> Alexandria, Virginia 22304
>
> Dear Mr. Chamberlain:
>
> A warm "hello" to you from Tennessee as you get settled in for your year at seminary. Just a few lines to let you know that we remember you daily in our prayers, and we hope all is well with you. Please let us hear from you whenever we can be helpful—you may feel that you are way off by your lonesome and we may be pretty busy, but never too busy to assist you in any way we can, and our thoughts are with you every step of the way. We, of course, look forward to your Ember Day reports

that will bring word of you and how things go with you.

As a junior, or first year student, please find a few enclosures: "Guide for Postulants and Candidates" and "Theological Studies and Examinations: A Syllabus" are sent on the request of the Examining Chaplains of this jurisdiction who are hopeful all theological students will use them and be guided by them. The pamphlets are rather hard to come by so we ask that you keep up with them. They should be most helpful to you in your preparation for the Ministry. The insurance letter is self explanatory and we enclose a copy of the diocesan Journal (sent separately because of postage rates) as it has all sorts of useful names, addresses and information should you wish to use it as a reference.

With very good wishes and warm regards,

It was signed by the secretary of the bishop of the diocese, printed on diocesan stationery, and dated September 3, 1968.

"What am I doing here?" David questioned. "Lord, are you sure this is what you want for me? This just doesn't feel right. God, give me a sign, some sign—please."

And at that moment, John walked through the door, saying, "Well, I think I'm through with what I'm going to do before dinner. How are you getting along?"

"I'm not yet," the Tennessean replied. "I'm still trying to figure out if I'm really here."

"I know what you mean," the Midwesterner snickered.

David began to unpack a few things while John took a seat on the bed. They chatted about leaving home and everything else that was behind them as they wondered what the next three years would bring.

But ever since John Harrison McCann had re-entered David Morrow Chamberlain's room, something was different—something was altered about the whole tone of their conversation.

For it seemed that as they talked of events that had taken place once upon a time and acknowledged the dramatic changes in their lives that going to seminary would bring, they found that because of a budding relationship, their feelings and thoughts were beginning to change—beginning to transition from ones of life and death to those of resurrection and new life.

CHAPTER 2

Four main halls made up the dormitory section of the seminary campus. Madison and St. George's Halls stood on the south side of the refectory, or dining room, running parallel to each other and connected by a guest quarters known as Moore Hall. St. John's and Wilmer Halls lay perpendicular to each other on the north side of the refectory.

After a couple of telephone calls to let families know that they had arrived safely, the Tennessean and the Missourian set out at 6:00 sharp on their first trek from Wilmer around St. John's to the dining hall. The two new "juniors" were quite assured by their own favorable first encounter that other suitable acquaintances awaited them.

The first meal at VTS proved to be a difficult occasion for mingling. Faculty members, students, friends, and family (and even a dog later to be dubbed affectionately as "the Hound of Heaven") packed the lounge area outside the refectory. If there appeared to be a focal point in the room at all, it was the person situated at a student council table, trying frantically to furnish everyone with a name tag.

Having been so adorned, David looked around the room at the people assembled and noticed that they came in all sorts and conditions of sizes, shapes, and ages—as probably would any group of assembled professionals-to-be. There was even a young deaf man in the crowd, busily engaged in the florid art of sign language with another gentleman.

After a bell rang someone said grace, and everyone entered the cavernous dining area filled with eight-place, institutional-style rectangular tables. Having greeted a few folks and subsequently having piled his plate high at the buffet, John located a seat and an adjacent one for David. The Missourian soon noticed, however, that his comrade had been re-routed to another spot by a middle-aged man, so he ate without his newfound companion, carrying on superficial conversations with those around him. John had decided not to become too engaged in dialogue, for he was keeping his eye on his watch so as not to miss Walter Cronkite's evening rendition of the news. That was assuming, of course, the television set worked—the one he had spotted in the common room of his dorm.

Later, after having been successful in that endeavor, the man from Missouri found himself back in his room, ready to resume the task of its organization. But what could actually be accomplished that evening was completed fairly quickly, so John headed back downstairs to see if he could continue talking with his new friend. As he headed for the Chattanoogan's room, the thought struck him that it would probably be a good idea to purchase his own TV, so the opportunity for his nightly news ritual might be guaranteed.

He found David busily ordering his own affairs and happy to see his new friend. David explained that it had been the dean himself who had sidetracked him at dinner. Dr. Jesse Trotter, who was also from Tennessee, wanted to reminisce a bit about old family connections and acquaintances.

Thus the new juniors resumed their conversation. They covered so many topics over the next two hours that it seemed hard to believe that only 120 minutes had clicked by. They filled their time by sharing a great deal of factual information about each other's backgrounds, and this is what each learned about the other:

David Morrow Chamberlain. Age: 21. Height: 5 feet, 9 1/2 inches. Weight: 140 pounds. Hair color: brown. Eye color: hazel. Build: medium. Accent: southern. Voice: tenor. Born in Chattanooga, Tennessee, he was an only child whose parents had divorced before he was two. David lived with his mother and grandparents in North Carolina until the age of ten, then moved back to Tennessee and attended both high school and college in Chattanooga. His father was a sports announcer for the Chattanooga Lookouts, a farm team for Seattle. David came directly from college into seminary. And he had a girlfriend named Patty Magill.

John Harrison McCann. Age: 23. Height: 5 feet, 10 1/2 inches. Weight: 170 pounds. Hair color: black. Eye color: brown. Build: stocky. Accent: mid-western. Voice: baritone with a hearty guffaw of a laugh—and he loved to laugh. Born in St. Joseph, Missouri, his mother worked as a housewife, his father was a psychology instructor, and he had one brother. After graduating from the University of Kansas and teaching English there for one year, he had set out for VTS.

If anyone else had overheard their conversation, he or she might have thought the details were from a newspaper obituary column, because there seemed to be so many facts and so little feelings. As they reviewed the events of their lives though, it became more and more evident that neither one of those two knew exactly what it was they were getting themselves into, as they began a new chapter in their lives. David was not even sure whether the end result of going into the ministry was really what he wanted to do with his life. John, however, was sure that he wanted nothing more.

Thus their relationship was born. And it was clear—just as the Christian faith promised—that new life was indeed emerging from old.

Robert Neal Redmon was exhausted. The drive from Houston, Texas, to Washington, DC, had worn him out, and his overweight condition had not helped him to weather the journey well at all. But his old, white sedan—"Flo," he called her—had made it just fine. She had been with him for a long time and had just completed her longest endurance run yet.

It was not so much the miles as it was her load that had been hard on Flo. And the extra weight was not so much caused by Bob's girth nor his clothes as it was by books and records. All those records! But that was Bob's passion. And even with the 442 albums he had managed to stuff in, he'd still had to leave four-fifths of his collection at home.

That collection had been valued recently somewhere in the thirty thousand dollar range and was known as one of the most extensive in all of Texas. So Bob understandably felt proud. He loved his music, and often it had been the one thing that had kept him going during the frustrating and lonely eight years he had taught English—years in which he had almost become an island unto himself.

That was not an unusual experience for Bob. While he was growing up, his lonely life as an only child had seemed to isolate him in a world for which he really did not feel suited. It was during that period that the church became a refuge for him. Bob had loved its ritual, its music, for as long as he could remember, and ultimately he knew that he wanted to offer his very life to the institution he adored. Finally, that dream had come to pass. He had enrolled in seminary.

Thirty-one years old! It was hard to be changing horses in mid-stream. But Redmon believed it to be the only option left open to him because he felt he had failed at everything else he had ever tried. A long trip it had been—in so many ways.

But as he emerged from his car at Wilmer Hall and surveyed everything he had to lug into his room, it seemed the longest journey still lay ahead. Fortunately, that room was on the ground floor and just inside the doorway, so at least he didn't have far to go. But after a couple of trips, he was sweating profusely, his 240 pounds weighing heavily on him—much too much girth for his five foot eight inch frame. But what could he do about that? He loved to eat (and to smoke) almost as much as he loved music.

His strawberry blonde hair glistened with sweat, and Redmon's glasses began to slide down his nose. Clearly he needed a break. Sitting in the middle of the floor of his dorm room, he was almost too tired to notice—but not so tired that he could not appreciate—an offer to help made by two visitors who introduced themselves as David and John. They had been talking in the room down the hall, which Bob thought he understood to be David's. The two had broken off their discussion and were thinking about perusing the neighborhood in search of a bite to eat when they heard other activity on the floor.

Bob's mouth turned up into a shy but pleased grin. He extended his hand in greeting and immediately accepted their kind offer of assistance. Thus, another new seminarian was welcomed to his home away from home. And then there were three.

Redmon began to unfold his own life story exuberantly, while Chamberlain and McCann reviewed theirs again. The conveyance of clothes, books, and records gave ample time for discourse, and it was not until about 10:30 p.m. that Flo was parked behind the dorm in order to spend the night near two small foreign cars.

Already, it seemed to Bob that his life was beginning to make sense again. In a way, he felt he was coming back to life, and he knew the relationship just commencing with his new acquaintances was something that he did not want to lose.

The three comrades continued to talk for a while longer, sharing beliefs and reasons as to why they were at seminary. Each one of them was very thankful for God's gift of the other two that day.

David seemed to be the quietest on the topic of why they all had come to VTS. Perhaps he was meditating on his thankfulness for these newfound friends. Silently he said to himself, "I believe in God. I know now that He believes in me."

As he thought of Patty and all the others whom he had left behind, it was clear to him that he would always cherish the hours, the memories, and the relationships of his past. But it was the unrealized ones of his future that he could finally, eagerly anticipate.

"I don't know what's out there, but I do know who's out there, and that 'who' loves me."

That comment from John caught David squarely in the middle of his contemplation, and brought him back to the present reality. The Tennessean sensed that he would be the most reflective of the three, given the kind of pensive aside he had just experienced in his own mind.

"It's not what you learn in life, it's how you learn it."

That second thought-provoking comment from John was not one with which Chamberlain necessarily agreed. It triggered the memory of his grandfather's sage, certain voice telling him many times, "Be careful what you learn; you can learn the wrong thing."

McCann's comment, however, was the sort of expression the other two would hear more and more from the Missourian, who was destined to be the most scholarly of the three.

"If Christ can die for us, then let us live for Christ," Bob chimed in with the kind of contribution that was to mark him as the most demonstrative of the trio—the one who would color his remarks with such superlatives that never left anyone wondering how strongly Redmon felt about anything.

And so it was after such a grand opening conversation that around 11:00 p.m., Flo was awakened from her thirty-minute rest period in order to provide transportation for three ravenous divinity students. Because of the lateness of the hour, their drive seemed almost endless before they found a store that was still open. It turned out to be a Seven-Eleven, which David had remembered passing earlier in the day on his initial trip to the campus. Sandwiches and drinks were consumed, as three postulants for Holy Orders began to progress from companionship to friendship.

They would never return to that Seven-Eleven. Their foray there served as a culmination of the events of that first night, which would always hold a very special place in their hearts. That was their beginning and, like birth itself, could never be repeated.

Chapter 3

For dormitory beds, the mattresses were not all that uncomfortable—well, not enough to lose sleep over anyway. So, the newly formed three musketeers felt fairly rested from their six hours of sleep when alarms went off at around 7:00 the next morning. It had been close to 12:30 a.m. when they got back from their snack the night before, and not wishing to part company quite yet, they had stayed up talking until about 1:00. The first full day was, indeed, to be fully packed, so they retired early in every sense of the word.

Upon reentering his room, David heard a knocking sound coming from his radiator. He was soon to realize that it was just John in the room above tapping on the pipes to say good night. David returned the gesture, smiling as he realized they had just begun a ritual.

John was still tapping the next morning, but the location had changed to one of the tables in the dining hall. He was not sure how anyone could stand to eat at that hour of the day. David and Bob were happy to take care of John's portion of food though—breakfast being David's favorite meal and any meal being Bob's. While those two stuffed their faces, John took time to carefully look around the refectory where they were to break bread together for the next three years. In all honesty, the dining hall looked like an airplane hangar—big, long, and wide with a high, arched ceiling that must have reached fifty feet from the floor. Probably there were fifty tables in the place, arranged in two rows of twenty-five. And along the walls were pictures, surely of people who had something to do with the seminary, deans and the like. There was a platform at the opposite end from the entrance with a podium, probably for announcements and such. John counted forty-six men and four women in the room.

Ted Boswell was there, along with several other members of the middler class who had come in early to help with orientation. But apparently the rest were newcomers. The three new friends had met a few of them either the night before or that morning on the way over to the refectory, but names had really not begun to sink in. John did remember two of the guys sitting at the other end of their table to be dorm mates named Bruce and Rich, but that was about as far as he had gotten. None of the others did he recognize.

When Bob and David finished eating, the three comrades returned to their respective rooms to pick up schedules for the day—schedules that had been printed specifically for the newest additions to the student body, which for that academic year was to consist of 178 men and 8 women.

Friday, September 6, 1968, would begin with a chapel service at 8:20. At 9:10, the members of the junior class and other new students were to meet with Dean Trotter and the faculty for orientation. After a coffee break at 10:00, that same group was to meet with Dr. Reid for presentation of the curriculum and registration procedure. Following that, a group picture would be taken. After lunch, each student would meet with the business manager, followed by the administration of a proficiency English test. After that, each student was to meet with his or her advisor for course selection.

The meetings were to take place in Aspinwall Hall—the building named for the New York brothers who had funded it—adorned with the tower that David had spotted upon arrival and could see from his dorm room. If the seminary quadrangle were a clock, Aspinwall sat at 12:00, the chapel at 1:00, Packard-Laird at 3:00, Sparrow Hall at 9:00, and the refectory surrounded by the four main dormitories at 6:00. The bookstore was located on the outside of the quadrangle behind Aspinwall.

Although the orientation sessions were spent sitting in those miniature desk-chairs, which bothered Bob's frame more than others, it was fairly standard fare. Most of the new students had already heard or read at least a brief history of VTS, but it was nice to hear some of the more memorable points reiterated.

In 1818 Francis Scott Key and others formed "An Education Society," a forerunner of the seminary. The Reverend William Wilmer was one of the first two professors in the early days of the institution—the same for whom our central figures' dormitory was named. In 1823 the seminary was formally established and opened in Alexandria. In the fall of 1827 the seminary moved to its current location, affectionately known as "the hill." The campus presently occupied just less than one thousand acres. Established in 1839, the Episcopal High School, located on land adjacent to the seminary, had always been closely associated with VTS. Expansion and improvement became the order of the day in 1947, and a successful building campaign in the fifties had provided money for the erection of new dormitories, faculty homes, and a library.

Virginia was decidedly Puritan in its early days with prejudice against the Roman Catholic system, so the school placed its emphasis not on the value of sacraments, but rather on personal piety, claim of duty, and scripture. But that did not mean that things were somber. It was refreshing to find that Dean Trotter, the chaplain, and other faculty members were quite human, and that seminary was proving to be more like a graduate school than a monastery.

The first thing with which the new students were presented was a document called "Character and Heritage of Virginia Seminary," best described as a matriculation statement. Every student was asked to read that document as printed:

> In the providence of God this Seminary was founded more than a century ago to train men for the ministry of Christ's Church. During its long life it has sought to fulfill this purpose, guided by a few clear principles of belief and action. In loyalty and devotion to these principles, its men have served the Church well at home and have carried the Gospel to other lands.
>
> This Seminary believes that its primary allegiance is to Jesus Christ. Its first duty is to know Him and to make Him known. It seeks to form lives of strong faith and true piety, fashioned and enriched with personal communion with Christ, and to make men able out of their own experience to preach Him to others as Lord and Savior. Christ must be put first. That is the Seminary's evangelical conviction, which . . . no other emphasis . . . may hide or minimize.
>
> The Seminary is Protestant both in its unwillingness to conform to any tradition or to heed any ecclesiastical claim that displaces the primary accent upon the Gospel, and in its readiness to accept new truth and to face the occasions of a new day. It

maintains the right of the individual Christian to his own personal relationship to God.

The Seminary is Catholic in its acceptance of the age-long inheritance of the Church in its Scriptures and Creeds, in its Sacraments and Orders. Its rule of discipline and worship it finds in the Book of Common Prayer and to this book it bids its members be loyal as the common order of this Church and as fruitful for Christian life and devotion.

This Seminary believes in the Church as the Body of Christ and the home of Salvation. It regards the Church also as a family of God's people in which all the members are called to live together in unity of mind and heart, in love and sacrifice, and in helpfulness and mutual esteem. Finally, the Seminary holds that life within it is not to be interpreted as private enterprise, but as a vocation into which its members are called by God, which is shared with others, and which asks for all that is best in them of work, personal living, faith and devotions.

Each student was then asked to acknowledge and accept those stated principles as representing the conditions under which theological education would be pursued at VTS. After having been given some factual information about the surrounding area, everyone took a coffee break. That wound up being as educational as the orientation, for therein numbers began to fall into place. The total enrollment that year represented fifty-four dioceses, including nineteen students who were not diocesan sponsored.

From all over the country and all over the world they had come. There were twelve from Texas, one from West Missouri, three from Tennessee, five from South Florida and two from Hawaii. They came to seminary from a wide body of backgrounds as well—military officer, college instructor, real estate agent, insurance agent, resort hotel manager, social worker, lawyer, salesman, bartender, bank teller, news reporter, psychiatrist, loan officer, case worker, hotel clerk, radio announcer, organist, florist, youth worker, short order cook, jazz musician, boys' home director, national fraternity field representative, school teacher, engineer, assistant to NASA administrator, minister of another communion, instructor to the deaf, Peace Corps volunteer, security guard, tennis instructor, restaurant manager, telephone company manager, book salesman, steel worker, ambulance driver, and funeral attendant.

The student-faculty ratio was eight to one. The married students outnumbered the singles two to one—those with a spouse living off campus.

Many lasting relationships were to be made over the next three years between the two sides of the marital fence. Special to David were Robert and Donna Sessum. Robert was also from the Diocese of Tennessee and a member of the middler class. His petite wife Donna was putting him through school by working as a medical secretary at the National Orthopedic Hospital. They had been married two years, having met at a Youth for Christ rally, and were interested in young people's work.

In the junior class there were Ken and Bambi Henry. Ken's father was the Bishop of the Diocese of Western North Carolina. Bubbly and cute Bambi taught that first year as a second grade teacher at a school in downtown Alexandria to help make ends meet. Also in the junior class were the Cunninghams and Wemberlys, but more about them later.

It was interesting to see the diversity of all the people who had come. Just as diverse were the number of people who had already left the place for service. VTS men were then serving in Africa, Asia, Latin America, the Caribbean, and islands in the Pacific. There was outreach to forty-nine dioceses in the United States, 25 percent of the present bishops were graduates, and 45 percent of the overseas bishops had been students at Virginia. There was a continuing education program, which brought back about eighty-five clergy a year. The administration had filled six new faculty posts recently, and with the continuing education program, campus definitely had an ecumenical flavor. As far as coffee hour was concerned, it had been an immensely profitable time to see how people and programs fit together.

At 10:30 the new junior class met with Dr. Richard Reid, the academic dean, who was to become one of their favorite professors. He seemed to overshadow the curriculum he presented—a curriculum that proved to be just what was expected at that stage of the game. The class would delve into an overview of biblical, linguistic, and theological studies. Beyond that, students were eager to hear about the field education program, which was in the process of being further expanded and more closely supervised. They were also interested in the clinical training program, which would take place during the summer between the first and second years. But those programs were eons away from where they stood on that day. So for the present time, they were quite content to be graduate students living in an academic world.

It was interesting to learn about the new Master of Arts in Religion program. As an alternative to the Bachelor of Divinity degree, the MAR degree was a two-year graduate level program for both men and women. That explained the eight women on campus, as well as four of the men. Theological education for those who were not seeking ordination had become a reality. The seminary also had a Master of

Systematic Theology degree. There seemed to be quite a number of different opportunities for people to explore their relationship with God.

After that meeting, John and David got their class pictures taken as fast as possible so that they could hurry off to the local shopping center down the road to open checking accounts. They almost had a wreck, for David was busy talking about the morning activities and looking at John instead of the road. John, who was looking at the road, saw potential danger ahead but couldn't remember David's name. But his "uhhing" and "ahhing" caused David to look ahead just in time to avoid taking them to the larger life. Consequently they arrived safely at the Seminary Plaza Shopping Center, which was to become their trading post for the duration of their time in Virginia. It wasn't a bad collection of stores really, because it afforded them the main conveniences of home—a bank, barbershop, Seven-Eleven, drugstore, grocery store, dry cleaners, and gas station.

There really was no need for them to obtain new state tags, or drivers' licenses, since technically they resided at a private institution. The only thing they needed to have for their cars was a sticker permitting them to use the seminary parking lot. Having found a place in said parking lot, they hurried to lunch in the refectory at the places saved for them by their fair-haired dorm mate, Bob.

In the dormitory hallway, there was a small rectangular cubicle for mail with slots assigned to each person. But the Redmon, McCann, and Chamberlain receptacles were empty that day, so they scampered over to meet with the business manager. It would seem that even God—at least learning about Him—had a price tag; thus, they reached for their checkbooks. John and David were fairly comfortable with what they had to pay, even though prices were high. Each

of them had a family that had set aside money for their education. But Bob, who was going through school compliments
of the Diocese of Texas, was feeling the pain of those costs
to his bishop. For a single student, the first year amounted
to $1,250. That total covered tuition, board, room, library
fee, and a one-time clinical training charge.

Of course, as with all institutions of higher learning, the
matriculation fee per student far exceeded the actual amount
needed for classes. For VTS, that expense was $2,800 apiece,
a price that only sounded low when later compared to a
figure almost double that amount, which would be charged
in the near future. Then there was hospitalization insurance,
graduation fees, a student activity fee, and books to buy.

The student activity fee paid for dances (which caught
David's eye), intramural athletics (which made John's mouth
water), and the library fee (which Bob could not begrudge).
Every student automatically became a member of the Missionary Society, organized in 1824—the medium through
which attention was drawn to church missions at home
and overseas. A student council elected by the student body
served as an informal forum for discussion of common problems, and the Student Aid Society helped out in emergencies
of a financial nature.

Then came the English proficiency exam, which really
was a bit of a farce for our central characters who had either
been English majors, taught English, or both. But the seminary community was made up of many different backgrounds,
and everyone did need to have at least a basic comprehension
of the language in order to meet admission standards.

In order to be enrolled in seminary, one either needed
to be a college graduate or at least be able to satisfy the
faculty that one was equal to the work of graduate school.
If a person did not have an undergraduate degree, then he

or she would work toward a certificate of competence rather than a bachelor's degree.

Admission requirements also included credentials supporting individual character and fitness for the ministry. Also required were a physical examination, a psychological evaluation, a letter of recommendation from one's bishop, a financial statement showing adequate resources to cover three years, and a satisfactory conference between the applicant and one or more members of the admissions committee.

With those requirements met, most people entered seminary as postulants for Holy Orders. But according to canon law, in order to reach the next step of candidacy, a statement was required from the seminary—a certificate of recommendation based on both scholastic and personal qualifications assessed by the faculty at the end of the first year. So with some hurdles jumped, and others yet to face, the three friends embarked on their new journey together.

At 4:00 they split up in order to meet with their individual advisors. For David it was Dr. John Rogers; for John, Dr. Holt Graham; for Bob, Dr. Fitz Allison. The basic thrust of those initial interviews was to establish a one-to-one contact between student and teacher, with particular emphasis on which academic courses would constitute one's seminary career. All three students felt they needed the basics at that stage of the game, so with only one elective permitted the first quarter, they all chose Dr. Mollegen's course entitled "Faith of Christians." That course was described as an advanced confirmation class, and its instructor was affectionately referred to as "Molle."

Bob signed up for that course just to hear Molle, having heard so much about him as a teacher for so long. David signed up for the course as an adult approach to Christianity, all of his church activity thus far having been more or less on a child's level—acolyte, junior choir, youth group, etc. John signed up for the course because it was the first one on the options list.

The time with the advisors went smoothly, but it would be interesting to note in the long run that all three would find their two closest faculty mentors to be the one teacher whose course they had just picked, Molle, and another whose course was required, Dr. Reid. Those professors would remain with them all three years as confessors, friends, faculty, spiritual leaders, teachers, and brothers in Christ.

With the day's schedule completed, it was time to rest and relax back in their rooms—and to begin to think about what possibly could be done to make their living areas more comfortable and colorful.

Friday night provided the first of many opportunities throughout the year for students and faculty to get together over dinner in the refectory. Supper that evening consisted of the specialty of the house—chicken as the main course and cheesecake for dessert. With all the trimmings, it took some time to get through that meal—except, of course, for John, who wasted no time in getting to the common room to hear Walter Cronkite give the nightly news. Bob and David remained, talking with fellow dormitory mates Bruce Myers and Rich Pocalyko until about 7:00. They then drifted out, glancing briefly at the bridge table and piano in the lounge where respectively Bob and David would spend many hours in the days and months to come. Having picked back up with John, they decided to stroll over to the chapel and get a good seat for the opening service that night.

Like a corpulent band major, Bob marched right down the center aisle to the third row on the epistle, or right, side. Though David and John followed quickly to sit with their friend, they would not have minded at all sitting a wee bit further back so as not to strain their necks looking up at the pulpit, but like everything Bob did, he did this with gusto. People gathered in pews and prayed their private prayers, then the service launched with a hymn.

From the opening notes, a shower of strong, clear voices mingled with the organ music, bathing the worshipers in notes and words that reverberated through the nave as though it were a holy sound chamber. The sensation encouraged everyone to sing just a little louder, to feel in his or her own chest the splendid resonance. As voices blended, so did hearts. The Christian faith that had brought them together began to take on bodily form. One could actually feel the presence of God and sense that the congregation already was becoming a community. David had walked into the chapel doubting that he belonged there, but in that instant he knew that whatever happened at seminary, he could count on things unfolding as they should.

After the opening prayers and scripture readings, the dean entered the pulpit. The 1968 entering class of Virginia Theological Seminary was about to be challenged with the ministry of the '70s.

Few indeed are the young men who enter a seminary these days with a conversion experience behind them. A far larger number enter because of an initial, driving interest in human issues, in social problems and welfare. They seek the resources of Christian

faith and insight to enable them to improve the
common lot of their fellow men. While in seminary
these men grow in understanding, commitment and
power. Only in time does the Church become for them
a central concern.

An equally large number of young men enroll in a
seminary from a sense of personal need for renewal.
Pressed by the riddle of life, they want to achieve
clarity at the center by finding themselves. They turn
to a serious study of theology to find a faith to live
by and a commanding purpose to serve. They seek
an answer to the question: how can I 'win through'?

In ways marvelous to observe, God takes in His
hand all of these men in their varied types and stages.
He clarifies motives, illumines minds, wins hearts,
and galvanizes wills—to make men His glad and
willing servants.

In preparing students to serve church renewal, the
faculty of this seminary is mindful that the majority of American people are thirty years of age and
under. Multitudes in this country in the lower age
range find the church archaic, and they tend to be
anti-institutional. For many the religious question
in life does not loom large. Theological education is
therefore undergoing rapid change in order that theological students may be prepared to communicate
persuasively and to win to the Christian faith the
new generations.

Within the lifetime and ministries of men now in
seminaries, eighty percent of the American people
will be living in urban-industrial complexes. In this
seminary very serious attention is being devoted to
church and society. The role of the Church. . . .

John's thoughts began to wander. He, as David had done upon his arrival at VTS, drifted off for a few moments to say to himself, "Well, here I am."

It was hard to believe that he was really, finally here. After applications to and rejections from both Nashotah House and General Seminary, hurried and harried phone calls to his bishop, and quick interviews with the faculty of VTS, finally he felt acceptance.

Acceptance—that was indeed the word that expressed what he felt to be blanketing the chapel that night. All of those people who sat in those pews, new and old, those who thought they knew what it was all about and those who so far had only been able to guess—that night they all felt they were accepted just as they were.

The dean continued:

> One would expect to find in the life of a dedicated seminary teacher a conviction that prayer is real and is to be practiced, that an immediate experience of God is possible, and that Almighty God cares more for people and justice among men than He does about books and obscure theological distinctions. I rejoice that Virginia has a faculty of convinced and committed Christian teachers of that sort.

Oh, that was good news for Bob. Though he was a teacher himself, and knew the value of books, still he knew all too well how sterile books alone could be. Books filled the hours. Books held knowledge, but they were not full of life. Books were entertaining, but one could not talk to them. Bob had found a home here. He returned his attention to the speaker.

The mysterious fact that God is found not only
in the light, in joy and in euphoria, but also that He
is found in darkness, in sadness, and in suffering
involves a dimension of mystery that is unwelcome
to many contemporary students. In recent years
a number of students withdrew from the seminary
when they were going through a thin time of it, going
through a period of inner struggle and darkness.
What a pity they left when they did! On the edge
of darkness they were in the very vestibule of the
Divine.

David thought of his grandmother, the one who had
meant so much to him, the one with whom he had lived and
shared life for so many years, the one who taught him so
much of what he presently called his faith, the one who had
died about a year ago. As he listened to the words of Dean
Trotter about darkness and light, sorrow and suffering, he
remembered his recent tears, shared with his mother and
grandfather. He understood the words of the dean because
he understood the meaning of loss. As sad as that time had
been, however, there was still faith and hope that she was
with God. In some mysterious way, he knew she was all right.

As the dean came to the end of his thoughts, David
looked around. Shifting his reverie from the family he had
left behind, he realized that he was in the presence of a
new family. He felt not only a sense of acceptance here but
of completeness—a sense of being surrounded with love, a
sense of new life and resurrection. He knew that it would
be more than enough.

Though they did not know it, the three new friends were
that night almost as close as they ever would be, for they all
were together at a new beginning. As chaplain Phil Smith

said the words of the 1928 Prayer Book Holy Communion service—words that they had heard so many times before— somehow they had a new sense of life, for the very simple reason that a new sense of life pervaded each one of them.

> The Body of our Lord Jesus Christ, which was given for thee, preserve thy body and soul unto ever-lasting life. Take and eat this in remembrance that Christ died for thee, and feed on him in thy heart by faith, with thanksgiving.
> The Blood of our Lord Jesus Christ, which was shed for thee, preserve thy body and soul unto ever-lasting life. Drink this in remembrance that Christ's Blood was shed for thee, and be thankful."

As Bob, David, and John knelt together at the communion rail crafted from African rosewood, they were one. They were one as friends, one with the memories of departed loved ones, one with the hearts and minds of loved ones who waited at home—one with the past, the present, and the future. One with God. As wafers of bread and sips of wine passed their lips, Christians were being born anew.

Chapter 4

It had been another long, hard, full day. It was not quite like the one before in that there was no travel involved—well, none by automobile anyway, but many miles had still been covered in mind. It's a funny thing about unfamiliar places. The first few days seem endless. Perhaps that is because there is so much to absorb and assimilate. So it was not surprising to discover that a certain three residents of Wilmer Hall did indeed sleep well that Friday night in their unfamiliar single beds.

They had not gone to sleep until 2:00 in the morning, for after chapel there had been a reception with refreshments in Scott Lounge outside of the refectory. After meeting a few more folks and logging in as many names as he could take in for one day, John suggested to his cohorts that they go out for a drink. Bob and David readily agreed, but not knowing the territory very well they decided to grab an old hand and invited Ted Boswell to come along. He accepted with pleasure, and the four soon found themselves at a place called The Red Lion. It was a quaint little bar and right in the same shopping center that they had designated as home base earlier in the day.

"Well, what do you think?"

Ted asked the question earnestly, even though he anticipated the conversation that followed. After a few drinks and much talk, it was decided that though there was definitely a system, organization, and cost to theological education, it was not quite the eschaton event to end all things that had been expected. So tipping their glasses to having survived the first full day, the four returned to the hill about 12:30.

Upon entering Wilmer Hall, they introduced themselves to two men talking inside. A middler from Ohio by the name of Henry Witten was raving about the pleasure and pain of the clinical training experience, which he had just gone through, to the young man whose attention he commanded.

That young man, almost hidden in a cloud of cigarette smoke, was Edward Lee Mullins, a twenty-seven-year-old member of the junior class from West Virginia, who had been a young executive with Humble Oil Company before deciding to enter the ministry. The conversation continued among them all with Henry doing most of the talking, a trait that seemed common to him. The three friends garnered enough details from the discourse to learn that Henry was president of his class, single, and an army sergeant who presently wrote insurance and who planned to return to military service as a chaplain.

At 2:00 a.m. the group finally broke up. Henry returned to his dormitory room in Madison Hall on the other side of the refectory, and Ed retreated to his room right next to David's in Wilmer. Before turning in, Ed wrote a letter home on his IBM typewriter, which he had been allowed to take from his previous job. Then he slowly drifted off to sleep to the static beaming from his prized color television.

Most of Saturday morning was spent back in Aspinwall, arranging class schedules with Dr. Reid, before taking a coffee break and then sitting in for a student council orientation. Their chosen classes for the first quarter looked good, partially because they were all in the morning, which left the afternoon open for study or other activities—like napping.

The academic quarter was to begin the following Monday at 9:10 following chapel with an introductory course on the basic biblical languages of Hebrew and Greek. Dr. Ross was to teach the five weeks on Hebrew and Dr. Reid, the five on Greek. Though there were many good commentaries and translations around, not only was there a necessity to have a beginning comprehension of those languages but some bishops adamantly required their students to learn the ancient tongues, including David's.

The Hebrew and Greek primer class repeated on Wednesday and Friday. At 10:35 in the morning on Monday, Wednesday, and Friday, a course in the Old Testament was offered by Dr. Newman, which basically covered the Pentateuch (the first five books of the Bible). At 11:35 on the same three days of the week, Dr. Mollegen convened the beginning course in systematic theology, the elective that had already been dubbed as an advanced confirmation class.

On Tuesday and Thursday mornings, they reported to either Dr. Reid or Dr. Mollegen for a class in New Testament, which was a basic sketch of the synoptic gospels—Matthew, Mark, and Luke. In addition, discussion sessions occurred every Tuesday afternoon for two hours beginning at 1:30.

The only other requirements for the members of the junior class were to attend a forum hour on current events held each Tuesday morning at 11:45 and participate in the seminary choir, rehearsals for which took place every Thursday afternoon at 1:30. Most of the classes convened in Aspinwall with only a couple of side trips nearby to Sparrow Hall and to Packard-Laird Auditorium.

Having finished with the morning activities, our three central figures decided to peruse the bookstore located behind the steeple-capped Aspinwall Hall, but after looking at the prices there, they decided to wait and see what was absolutely necessary for purchase before laying down cash. So after the customary Saturday hamburger lunch, and with no particular desire to work on their rooms, they decided to get a glimpse of the seminary's environs.

One of the advantages of VTS was its proximity to the nation's capital. Thus it served not only as a focal point for all sorts and conditions of men preparing for the ministry, but also as a melting pot for meetings and speakers from all over the world. As Bob, David, and John headed for Arlington Cemetery to see the Tomb of the Unknown Soldier and John F. Kennedy's grave, they counted themselves lucky to attend a school near the nation's capital and grateful as well to be Americans.

They also had time to see the National Archives in the District of Columbia, walk the streets of Georgetown, and grab a bite to eat. But with the activities of three hard days having caught up with them, they decided to defer their explorations until the following afternoon.

The sun ascended over the seminary on the Thirteenth Sunday after Trinity. It was another hot, late summer day and, like every Sunday, a hard morning for the kitchen staff, since that was the only day when breakfast was served twice. There was one offering at 7:15 and another at 8:15 because the middlers and seniors left at different times to reach their assigned field work.

The later breakfast found our friends talking with Ed, the ex-Humble Oil exec, and several others among their older colleagues regarding feasible places to consider for their own field work placements next year. There really was no hurry about it, so the conversation was pretty relaxed as far as David, Ed, and John were concerned. In fact they would have been just as content to spend the morning visiting a favorite off-day locale affectionately referred to by seminarians as "St. Mattress on the Springs." But Bob, being quite Anglo-Catholic, would not think of missing a Sunday worship service, nor would he allow his cohorts to skip, so it appeared that the day would be tailored to Bob's dictates.

Grace Church, Alexandria, seemed to have just the right amount of flavor to suit Bob's taste. Flo soon found herself following well laid out directions into the suburbs around the seminary. Having located the beautiful brick church, Bob felt right at home in a service complete with sanctus bells and incense—Holy Communion. As far as Bob was concerned one really couldn't call it church without Holy Communion.

The other three, being of a lower church variety, were not as adamant about the style of service. That was especially true for Ed, who found himself at quite the opposite end of the worship spectrum from Bob, having come from the very "low" Diocese of West Virginia. The difference was so dramatic that later in the week when the two entered the chapel together, Bob genuflected and Ed almost tripped over him. In a state of bewilderment Ed asked Bob what he had dropped.

The service that morning at Grace Church was somewhat sparsely attended, and enthusiasm was not at all evident in the singing of the opening hymn. In fact, the four felt out of place singing as loudly as they did but Bob's beautiful tenor voice led them on. Apparently the congregation's lack of luster was evident to the rector too, for as the congregation began the sermon hymn in the same vein, he stopped the choir, organ, and congregation short to announce that they were going to sing the hymn over and this time do it right.

"If you don't," he said, "you're going to hear the longest sermon you've ever heard."

Needless to say, the singing then swelled to meet Bob's standards.

After the service, having perused a copy of the Washington Post for amusements, and with Ed otherwise engaged, the original team of three hurried through their Sunday afternoon chicken dinner so that they could take a nap, work on their rooms, and still have time to walk the streets of Washington D.C. before the academic grind began the next day. However, by the time they were ready to leave the grounds, the evening hours were upon them.

Sunday dinners were not a great treat at the refectory— normally leftovers from the past few days. So they decided to start in Georgetown with dinner at Old Europe, and then, at David's suggestion, take in a $3 movie at one of the theaters of the Loew's chain in DC. Throughout the meal, David's compatriots were impressed by his exceptional love of movies. When they asked him how he came to be such a fan of films, he shrugged.

"I guess I've loved movies since the very first one I saw with my mom back in 1951—*Cinderella,*" he said. "My parents divorced when I was two, and they lived in different states so I have fond memories of going to the movies with each of my parents separately, and once—to see *The Bridge on the River Kwai*—with both of them together. I'll never forget that," he smiled.

"And I always think of my dad when I see *The High and the Mighty*, he remembered, because of all the films we saw, that was our favorite."

"That's one of my favorites too," said John.

"Movies are a great escape," said David. I love the way I can walk into a theater and be conveyed to another time and place, even another world. Isn't it amazing how the very same viewing room can transport you into infinite adventures—a sci-fi thriller or a love story or a guns-blazing western—just by watching images flashing on that big screen."

Everyone enjoyed the movie that night even more than usual since they were appreciating it through David's eyes.

Coming out of the theater at about 10:00, the new friends found that they were not all that far from the Washington Monument and decided to walk over and see the grounds. Under an indigo blue canopy of twinkling stars and with a gentle breeze blowing off the Potomac, it was not long before they had settled onto their backs in the grass beneath the memorial to stare up at the heavens. It was exciting to think that the creator of those heavens was to be the subject of their studies for the next three years. Hopefully they would begin to comprehend more and more that God, as impossible a task as that might seem to any human mind. But if they were to be messengers of the divine, messengers to men, ministers of His church, and Episcopal priests, then that was the subject matter they had to learn as intimately as the proverbial back of their hands.

That was the central motivation that they all shared even though their methods would differ—as they do for all those whom the Lord calls into His service. Perhaps it is the truest proof of the presence of the third member of the Trinity, the Holy Spirit of God, that He deals differently with His subjects, calls them into different service, works through them individually, and smiles as they respond differently to His call to proclaim His message of saving grace to all the world.

If that were not the case, then the conversation about to

take place wouldn't have. God very often invites us into a fuller understanding of both Him and one another by allowing us to share our differences. In that way risk, change, growth, friendship, and commitment have room to flourish in a way that otherwise might not be possible.

"Question: Are you two all that sure that you want to go into the ministry for the rest of your lives?" asked David.

His inquiry literally stumped Bob and left him unable to express himself except to peer at David over the top of his glasses with wide-eyed consternation. For him, the only reason to be in seminary was to prepare for the ordained ministry. What other reason was there? But John had a verbal answer for David.

"Yeah, I'm sure," he said.

"How do you know you're sure?" David retorted. "Do you feel called by God, as they say?"

"I don't know if I'd say 'called by God' as in a conversion experience sort of way," John returned. "My certainty comes more by nature of the fact that I've never really wanted to do anything else. I guess in a way that's a call."

David's mind drifted back to the moment at Daytona Beach just after high school graduation in 1964. Having lost his contact lens the night before in the grass near the beach, he had risen that next morning unnaturally early for someone who was not a morning person—at 5:45 a.m. to be exact—and he did that without benefit of an alarm, to boot—to search again for the plastic disc. As the sunrise bloomed golden orange over the dark, mysterious sea, David had stopped in his tracks, spellbound by the beauty of God's creation.

At that moment he became aware of a presence approaching him. Even though there was no one else around, David knew absolutely that the invisible presence was real and that it was moving toward him. He also knew without doubt that he was in the company of God. As the presence surrounded him, he began to tremble. Oddly he was not afraid. Indeed, he felt a great sense of peace, as well as confirmation that his recent decision to give his life to the Lord's service was exactly what God wanted him to do. In a few moments, the presence passed; his shaking ceased. He turned, walked ten steps, knelt down, and picked up his contact lens lying in the grass.

"OK, John," David said, "but how exactly do you want to serve God—to serve His people? Aren't there other ways to serve other than through the institutional church?"

At that point Bob found his entrance line.

"Well, the institutional church is God's people. That is how we serve God and His people on Earth—by committing ourselves to the service of the church."

There was silence. Bob had said his piece. John was in agreement with Bob, but felt that David wanted more as far as a definition of "the church" was concerned, and John was wrestling with just how to say it. David was indeed wrestling with just that very thing and in a few more seconds confirmed John's suspicions.

"Well, I guess I could say that I have a call to serve God," David continued. "I don't really think I would have taken all that time to fill out all those forms, see all those people, make all those applications, and ultimately drive all those miles if I didn't feel in some way that I wanted to commit my life to God. But I certainly didn't come all that way convinced that I wanted to spend the rest of my life in what we call 'the church.'"

Bob sputtered, "But how else can you possibly live out that commitment?"

"That's exactly what I'm asking you," David pointed out. "I am saying that because I'm in seminary that I want to commit my life to God, that I want to serve Him and His people with my life. But am I trapping myself into a profession that I don't necessarily want to buy into?"

John found his words. "No, I don't think you are selling yourself down the river, so to speak. I don't think you are committing yourself to anything that you can't get out of just because you want to go to seminary and prepare yourself for serving God. The way you do that might be in a pulpit or it might be by managing a movie theater somewhere." (John felt proud of himself for bringing in the movie reference.)

"What you're saying, David, is that you're not sure you want to be a priest?" Bob queried.

David replied, "No, I'm not sure I am saying that, Bob. I may feel in three years that I want to be a priest, but that I still don't want to be tied down to . . . to . . . the . . . uh . . ."

"The parish ministry," John posited. "I think that's what you're trying to say. You're not sure if you want to be tied down to the parish ministry. You want to serve God. You probably want to serve Him by being a priest. But you're just not sure that you want to do it by serving in the parish ministry."

Bob frowned. "But what other type of ministry, real ministry, is there but the parish ministry?"

"Well," David added, "then tell me just exactly what the parish ministry is. OK, I want to serve God. I may even want to be a priest. But what really is this parish ministry bit? The only knowledge I have of it is from what I see in my rector's work at my home church. I see him conduct the service. I hear him preach. I know he visits in homes and in hospitals and teaches Sunday school. I know that's only a limited view of what he does every day probably, but from what I see, I'm not sure that's what I want to spend my life doing. Maybe you're right, John. Maybe I just want to learn to serve God—or accept the fact that I can serve Him—as a theater manger. Does any of that make sense?"

"I understand," Bob chimed in, "but for me, the church is my life. It has been my whole life long—and through some rough years as an only child and as a lonely school teacher. At times when I had nothing else to hold on to, with nothing else to love or live for, the church was there, giving me meaning. I guess what I'm saying is that I want to in some way return the favor. The church has given me life. I want to give my life back to it. If that means preaching and celebrating and calling on parishioners, okay, fine; that's not important. Well, it is important, because I consider myself to be an Anglo-Catholic. I love the Holy Communion, and I love it done right, and that's how I'm going to do it."

"But that doesn't contradict what you said, Bob," offered David. "You want to do it because it has given you life, and you want to offer your life by conducting worship the best way you know how. I really can plug into that, Bob. We're actually talking about the same thing. We're talking about living our lives the best way we know how as a gift to Him who gave life to us. The only place we differ is that you're sure you want to live out that gratitude in the life of the institutional church. I'm just not sure that's the way I want to live it out."

Then it was John's turn to feel stumped. As he listened to the discourse going on between his two colleagues, he wondered just how he fit into the scheme of things they were discussing. The ministry had indeed been something that he had always wanted to do, but why? Was that out of any great commitment to God, or out of any great desire to return his life to the One who had allowed His Son to die on a cross for him? This Lord that his friends were talking about seemed to be one that lived in their hearts, causing them to act. But the Lord they were talking about, he had always been a little bit reticent to accept. He knew he did not buy into the necessity of an overly emotional experience in order to be a Christian. He had always been turned off by the type of person who would come up to him on a street corner asking, "Have you been saved, brother?" He had always wanted to respond, "Saved from what?" John continued for a while longer in thought.

"What are you thinking about over there?" asked Bob.

"Yea, what's going on?" David asked.

John expressed the thoughts that had been going through his mind. He went on to say that he defined himself as a Christian and as a believer, but he did not see himself necessarily as one who was supposed to give his life for his faith. He was just doing what he wanted to do, and what he had always wanted to do.

"For instance," John commented, "I've always wanted to stand at the altar and celebrate Holy Communion. I've always wanted to work with young people, and especially in this day and age, that desire is there all the more. But whether that's a call from God, or a giving of my life for my faith, I'm not sure I can say that—or at least I'm not sure I can say it yet. All I know is that's what I want to do."

And so it was. Three young men lay beneath the Washington Monument on a late summer evening in 1968. They were beginning their seminary careers as members of the junior class. One was from Texas, one was from Tennessee, and one was from Missouri—three states and three states of mind. One considered himself to be committed to God, one considered himself committed to His church, and one considered himself committed to His service. Those were distinctions one might not ordinarily draw about the ministry, they all seeming to be aspects of the same thing. But for

David Chamberlain, John McCann, and Bob Redmon, they were distinctions that needed to be made right then and right there. Whether or not those would change remained to be seen.

The only "given" was that seminary lay ahead for three new friends, and three different reasons existed for that beginning. If one lesson had been learned on the grounds of the Washington Monument that night, it was that not everyone came to seminary for the same reason. That had been attested to in the sermon a few nights before, but it took a night under the stars for them to actually comprehend that fact on a personal level. What lay ahead was unknown, as the future always is. But together, the three new seminarians were beginning that quest. Of that much, they were sure.

At the end of the first day of classes on Monday, September 9th, David wrote a letter to Patty. He told her all about the layout of his room, the events of the past four days, the classes for which he had registered, and the new relationships that had already begun, including one with a deaf student who that very day had begun to teach them sign language. He pledged to her his desire to take all that had brought him to that point in his life and build on it. Then with an expression of his love for her, he closed with a benediction from the book of Genesis:

"The Lord watch between you and me, when we are absent one from the other."

CHAPTER 5

Classes raced into their second week. Already the eschaton event of the first graduate school test bore down on the junior class. It really was nothing that any final grade would rest on, just one of Dr. Newman's famous content quizzes in Old Testament. But since it was the first exam, every junior was cramming like mad.

Roy Donald Green Jr. sat down at his desk in St. George's Hall for the third time that Tuesday night, a diploma in biology from the University of Florida hanging on the wall above him. The paragraphs of literature before him were quite different from the pictures, diagrams, and lab work with which he had specialized in college. A long night of memorization of historical facts, people, places, and events that made up the fact-laden book of Genesis weighed heavily on his mind.

In the past week and a half as seminary life settled into a normal routine, he found that he really did enjoy quiet time in his room studying. He would normally stay there from just after dinner until the nightly hall prayers at 10:30, diligently perusing and committing to memory what had been the meat of the day's study. It was a fairly consistent schedule, one broken up only by the regularly scheduled Thursday evening community worship service and an occasional social foray.

His room was like all the others—clean but plain. He had already spent some time considering what color of bedspread, what assortment of towels, what size of carpet, and what arrangement of books would give his quarters the look that he wanted. Roy was the type of man who looked older and more mature than his twenty-one years made him. He naturally commanded the respect of others, and his personal space would soon reflect that.

It really had been a last minute decision that brought Roy to seminary. He had always thought that he would be a doctor. But one day in church the thought just hit him in a moment of prayer: "I wonder what it would be like to be a priest?"

Call it divine intervention. Call it what you might, but Roy—all six feet four inches and 230 pounds of him—was on his way to ordination from the Diocese of Central Florida.

Staff, faculty, and students had already noted his commanding presence. His laugh rang out, his eyes sparkled, and people genuinely felt comfortable around him. Being as handsome as he was, Roy had no trouble meeting and greeting and getting acquainted with other people in seminary, especially the eight women who were part of the campus scene. All of them were quite attractive, and the Floridian hoped that he would indeed get the chance to know each one of them a little better.

And Roy generally felt comfortable around almost everyone he encountered, whether over a cup of coffee after class or at one of the three daily meals. But he found that he enjoyed himself most when around three particular characters from Wilmer Hall. Bob, David, and John already had become known as cut-ups because of their comic rendition of Genesis, which they were putting together as a way to prepare for the upcoming quiz. It was a routine that had everyone splitting their sides with laughter, including Roy and even the deaf student, James Francis Alby, who received the gist of it in sign language.

Jim was from Wisconsin and had been a complete stranger to sound his entire life. Because he had been in the breach position at birth, his doctor had to turn him using forceps, and in so doing he destroyed Jim's auditory nerves. Nevertheless, Jim had found his passion in life, which was to be a teacher. Knowing that he would have a hard time keeping up in class because of his deafness, he needed to find someone in class who took good notes and then copy them. That man was Bob Redmon.

It seemed as though the two had little in common. Bob, who arrived on campus lugging a portion of his prized record album collection, was never found in his dorm room without classical music pouring out of his open door. Meanwhile Jim was locked in lifelong silence. But the two of them were made for each other.

It was uncanny how Bob could write so neatly and still get more information in an organized form than could any of his colleagues. But then he had been a teacher for many years, and one thing those years had taught him was how to be a good student.

Since Jim was not a great lip reader, he relied on sign language. That necessitated either finding others who knew or could learn the hand signals or Jim was left out of all social interaction. An upperclassman who was proficient in sign language agreed to meet Bob, David, and John on Monday nights to teach them the alphabet symbols. Once they learned how to spell words out, they could learn shorthand gestures from Jim.

When Jim became friends with Bob, he scored a "three-for-the-price-of-one" by also landing the company of David and John. Because the three hearing friends learned how to communicate in Jim's language, he was able to have a front and center seat when the three broke into a comedy routine. And on that evening before the first exam Jim, along with the affable Roy and the ex-oil exec Ed, enjoyed the best seat in the refectory for Bob, David, and John's comic rendition of Genesis, which our three main characters had nearly completed. Seated around one of the dining tables were six people: our three authors, plus Ed, Roy, and Jim. All were laughing at the final version of what had come to be known as "Genesis: Once Over Lightly."

"In the beginning, God tripped over the earth, and said, 'Let's get some lights on around here.'"

After David read the first line of the text, Bob and John picked up the story, continuing through the tale of Adam passing the buck to Eve and Eve passing the buck to the serpent. On and on it went as they took turns reading the comic version while one of them communicated in sign language to Jim. Everyone was laughing so hard, that others drifted over from nearby tables to hear the rendition. It finally broke up with requests for a similar rendition when they got to Exodus.

Jim departed for his room on the first floor of St. John's, the dorm that connected Wilmer to the dining hall. Ed and John adjourned to their respective places to watch the news. But David lingered for a while at the piano in Scott Lounge, in order to practice his amateur improvisations. The first selection of the night was "Jesu, Joy of Man's Desiring" which didn't sound half bad when joined by Bob's tenor and Roy's bass on the vocal parts.

David closed out their musical interlude with an invitation to Roy to come by later for a visit and then stay for Johnny Carson's monologue on *The Tonight Show*, which they normally watched in color in Ed's room. Roy accepted gladly and departed St. George's a little after 11:00 following the evening's hall prayers, the leadership of which was rotated among the dorm members.

To get from St. George's to Wilmer, one had to cut diagonally across the courtyard in front of the dining room. As he did so, Roy noticed the abundant trees that surrounded the dormitories and the sound of the crickets chirping. Although it was the middle of September, summer was still in the air. Lights began to blink off in several rooms above his head; some were already dark. But in those areas reserved for the junior class, midnight oil was still burning in a late effort to meet Dr. Newman's requirements for the next day.

As Roy entered Wilmer Hall, Bob Redmon's room was the first one on the left. Although it had only been a few hours since they last spoke, still Roy was courteous enough to knock on the door to say hello. Listening to a Mahler symphony, Bob was parading around his room clutching books and notes. Roy took a minute to savor the music, being a classical fan himself. He couldn't help but notice that Bob had yet to do very much with his room. The bookcase was piled high with reading material, the record player was sitting on the floor with several albums leaning up against it, and the bed sheets tangled. Aside from the things that had actually come with the room, the only addition was a new rocking chair sitting in one corner.

"How's the studying going?" Roy asked.

The occupant of the room looked up and groaned. Roy chuckled and headed down the hallway to his destination, the next to the last room on the right. In total contrast from Bob's room at the other end of the hall, David's room was neat and in good order.

David was seated just inside the doorway at his desk on the right, which faced the wall—a desktop completely free of any material except for the book that he was studying. The remainder of the furniture was arranged efficiently along the walls, leaving a large open space in the middle of the room. Added for color were two small green throw rugs and two seascapes on the wall.

"Greetings," the Tennessean uttered, welcoming the tall Floridian to his abode. "What do you think of my new home?"

"OK," Roy replied. "The pictures add a nice touch. Where did you get them?"

"People's Drug Store—$4.95 a piece."

"Thought anything about an area rug instead of the little ones?" the Floridian opined. "I think I'm going to get one."

"I probably will," replied the resident, "but I want to shop around a little more. After that, though, I think I'm pretty well done fixing things up."

About that time Bob wandered in, still clutching his notes. In his most professorial voice he began naming the six sons of Keturah (one of Dr. Newman's pet questions about the book of Genesis, though its relevancy to any aspect of ministry in the future was seriously questioned by just about every seminarian on campus).

"Zimran! . . . Jokshan! . . ."

In the middle of Bob's recitation, John jogged into the room, winding up his daily exercise routine by counting his final steps.

"Medan! . . . Midian!" Bob continued, but John counted louder and louder just to see what kind of response he could get.

"5,987! 5,988!"

"Shuah!" Bob bellowed as he nudged John over to David's bed, pushed him down, and sat on him.

"Now keep quiet until I finish this list," the Texan ordered. "Ishbak!"

"Help, I can't breathe!" the man from Missouri feigned from the Land Down Under.

David and Roy were so entertained by the antics of their friends that they almost missed Ed's summons from next door to join him for the beginning of the program they had come to watch.

"Here's . . . Johnny!" As announcer Ed McMahon's voice rose to crescendo, they all filed over to Ed's. The comic relief evaporated everyone's stress, but they parted company at the conclusion of Carson's monologue in order to get in one more review of notes before going to bed.

As Roy strolled back to St. George's Hall, something bothered him. Although he enjoyed the company of the guys in Wilmer, it was obvious that those three had already bonded as a group. Bob and David and John clearly were a team, and it would be hard for anyone else to break into that circle of friends. He wondered if Ed felt the same way.

Roy knew that he would enjoy the time he would have together with all the Wilmerites—to talk, to argue, to discuss, to share, and to learn. But he also knew that in order to experience the type of closeness that at least the three of them had found, he would have to look elsewhere.

Dr. Newman's quiz came as no great cataclysmic blow to the members of the junior class. They had prepared sufficiently. In fact, the only real surprise of the hour was when the middlers paraded into the classroom just before

the examination in order to serenade their lower classmen
with a funeral dirge. It was a ritual that had been practiced
for years and would continue so to be, just before that first
test was given each fall.

To no one's surprise, the first question on the exam
required them to name the sons of Keturah, followed by
the sons of Leah, and then the rest of Jacob's children. A few
definitions closed out the quiz, so that it really did not take
much more than about twenty minutes to finish. All of them
thought they had fared well, including Ed who expected to
receive his usual "C." Bob, David, and John each made an
"A," as did Roy.

So it was of that sort of news to date that the first Ember
Day letters (quarterly reports to one's bishop) were comprised. Those were opportunities for the seminarians to check
in with their ecclesiastical authorities to let them know how
seminary life was going.

David composed his letter basically around the theme of
thanking the Right Reverend John Vander Horst for his guid-
ing influence in sending him to Virginia. Up to and through
his college days, the only seminary with which he had been
familiar was at Sewanee, Tennessee. But the bishop had
felt that for him to go there would place all of his higher
education within too small a geographical area—only fifty
miles wide to be exact. So the bishop suggested that David
look at either VTS or General Seminary in New York.

David reported that he was pleased with the decision
he had made. He pointed out that all with whom he had
been associated seemed to have a united purpose in serving
the Lord, but he did not go into the discourse of the night
on the grounds beneath the Washington Monument as to
exactly how differently living out that purpose might be.
He described the beauty of the campus and his belief that

he had chosen the right place for his theological education. And, he added, the people there were warm and friendly.

Closing out his Ember Day letter with facts like meeting the deaf student, David noted that he already felt at home and hoped that the rest of his seminary experience would go as well as the first few days. He thanked the bishop for all he had done and meant, and closed the letter with the same benediction from Genesis with which he had closed Patty's.

Ed and David, living next door to one another, had found themselves growing closer as they shared bits of news from home, their diocese, and other places. So David asked Ed to read his letter to the bishop. Ed had become aware of David's sensitive way of putting things, but he thought his young friend might be assuming too much to use the same kind of benediction with his prelate that he had used with Patty. David thought not. So they agreed to disagree.

Bob spent most of his letter on financial matters, including some insurance concerns. That really was the only place his letter differed from John's, which was more or less a report of classes being taken, advisor's name, and a request for dispensation from the study of Greek.

That New Testament language was still on the books as a requirement, but more and more bishops were letting their seminarians off the hook as far as the study of Greek was concerned because of the number of good translations available and the fact that time could probably be spent in more worthwhile endeavors. Dispensations were being requested and granted right and left. As has already been noted, however, that was one place where David had to part company with his friends, for Bishop Vander Horst was adamant that students have a working knowledge of the language in which the New Testament was written. David therefore had resigned himself to the study of Greek.

The postulants from Tennessee were informed of the position of the diocese on the study of Greek, as well as other policy points, in the two pamphlets that had followed the letter of greeting on the day they arrived at seminary. In fact, those two pamphlets comprised the first packet of mail that David had found in his cubicle in the hallway.

Mail was delivered daily to each cubbyhole by a member of the dorm designated as the person who was to lead hall prayers, which were offered the first three nights of each week. That mail was obtained from what surely was the smallest post office in the United States, a tiny building on the Seminary Road side of the campus, operated by a large, lovely lady named Dot Bliss.

With Ember Day letters sent, things slowed down for the weekend. Even though there was another content quiz scheduled for the next Wednesday, that one to cover the book of Exodus, the Wilmerites did not feel as if it was yet time to worry. As Henry Witten, the army sergeant- turned-insurance-writing seminarian, was fond of saying: "If it's not tomorrow, why worry about it. And if it is tomorrow, it's too late to worry about it."

Besides, they already had one exam under their belts, as well as some idea of what tests were going to be like in seminary, so they no longer feared the unknown.

As Thursday night approached, the waiters assigned for dinner in the refectory had been recruited from St. John's Hall. Bob, David, and John were seated at the table served by Jim Alby, who had reserved their seats. Jim enjoyed the company of the three and was feeling more and more at home as their companionship began to penetrate more and more the barrier of deafness that encased his silent world.

No one was made more aware of that silent world than David that night after everyone had sat down and begun dinner. A few minutes later, the dean clinked a glass to make an announcement, and David turned to Jim to spell it out, only to realize that Jim was continuing to eat his meal. Jim of course had never even heard the clinking of the glass. David was amazed to realize the number of things that he took for granted.

Progress in other relationships was also being made. It being another faculty night, teachers and students were enjoying the company of one another again in the weekly opportunity for the community to bond as a family before all went to chapel for Holy Communion.

At the Alby table, the students were happy to have Dr. Mollegen seated with them, the wise professor who was becoming everyone's favorite. It was nice to get to know him better, only to see him in a different light just a little later as he led the service with Dr. Reid and Dr. Stanley. By that night, it had become apparent how the chapel services were scheduled. There was an assigned minister of the week who led worship each morning, performed one duty on Thursday evening, and held a different responsibility the following Thursday evening. Middlers and seniors served as readers and chalice bearers for the weekly evening service. And if a student was not serving with a teacher, he was probably sitting with one in the pew. Those opportunities gave Thursdays a solid block of time for faculty-student rapport.

A new ritual was beginning to take place either immediately after the chapel service or a little later in the evening. That was to gather as many as were interested for a trip to one of the local restaurants for a late snack. There were several spots vying for top attendance honors, but the favorite quickly became a place called Lums. The place specialized in hotdogs boiled in beer, which was popular to many. Another specialty, called the "Lumburger," was their version of a

Sloppy Joe. Ted Boswell, the middler who was already experienced in where to go and where not to go, had introduced
the men from Wilmer Hall to that establishment.

The other popular nightly diversion—especially on the
weekends—was to find a good late show on television and
pop some popcorn or bring in a pizza from one of the local
parlors. The showing of *Ivanhoe* started that tradition. Roy
returned to Wilmer Hall for the color presentation in Ed's
room, and Chuck's Carry-Out supplied the pizza. (More
about Chuck's later.)

The middlers officially welcomed the junior class through
the student council picnic, which was held on Saturday afternoon, September 21st, in Trotter Bowl. The occasion gave the
single folks a good opportunity to mingle with the married
couples, who were never seen in the dining room at dinner.
David got to visit with fellow Tennessean and junior Carl
Cunningham and his wife Nelia, as well as middler Robert
Sessum and his wife Donna. Bob and John conversed with
fellow class members Don Wimberly and wife Wendy from
Louisiana and Ken Henry and his wife Bambi from North
Carolina. Tradition required the married couples to bring
the sandwich meats and singles to supply the condiments.
Everyone seemed to enjoy themselves, and it felt good to see
a larger community beginning to form.

A few days later, David wrote another letter to Patty.
Once again he brought her up to date on the decor of his
room which now included the two seascapes and the more
recent acquisition of a full area rug. Also, he went into some
detail about the events that had occurred since his last letter,
including how popular the comic renditions were of Genesis
and Exodus, and he noted as well that it seemed everyone
was beginning to feel more comfortable and settled. David
talked a little bit about classes, especially Dr. Mollegen and

how special that particular faculty member was becoming to everyone. A remarkable teacher without question, the students were calling him, often quoting one of the professor's most memorable lines: "Christ meets man's sin like the irresistible force meeting the immovable object."

David also mentioned how close his relationship was becoming with John and Bob, as well as more and more with Ed next door. Then since the Wilmerites were waiters for the week, and it was about time to report for duty, he signed off with another expression of his love for her and closed with the following: "The memories of the past I will always cherish, and the unrealized ones of the future I eagerly await."

CHAPTER 6

The year 1968 had already been marked by turmoil and confusion. In January North Vietnam launched the bloody Tet Offensive against American-backed South Vietnam. The awesome attack shocked American leaders into reconsidering their strategy in striving for an outright win over North Vietnam and to seek instead a graceful way to exit. In April the assassination of Martin Luther King Jr. in Memphis rocked the nation to its core. And in June a killer gunned down presidential candidate Robert Kennedy in Los Angeles.

With such events as those as the setting, the Archbishop of Canterbury convened the Tenth Lambeth Conference in London in July. This assembly of Anglican bishops from around the world came together once a decade to discuss global concerns. As the American branch of the Anglican Communion, the Episcopal Church sent its prelates to join with their brothers in Christ that summer. The agenda reflected the social issues of the day, especially regarding women in the ministry. The conference eventually recommended the ordination of women as deacons but found the arguments for and against women in the priesthood to be "inconclusive."

In those uncertain times, the junior class of the Virginia Theological Seminary gathered for its initial retreat at the

Episcopal Conference Center off I-95 in Roslyn, Virginia, just north of Richmond. The first weekend in October had been set aside so that the members of the new class and their professors might have time away from the hustle and bustle of the academic life to begin to both focus on and wrestle with their own personal and vocational concerns. A two hours' drive from the quiet, green seminary campus, the conference was scheduled to begin on a Friday evening with dinner at six o'clock.

The three Wilmerites, along with Jim Alby but without Ed Mullins, allowed plenty of time to pile into Bob's aging, white sedan, Flo, and head south for the overnight event. On the way down they decided that David and Jim would room together, and Bob and John would share quarters. As bags were dropped and beds were made, Bob and John could be heard amicably arguing in their room over who got the larger of the two beds. Trying to contain his laughter at what was going on across the hall, David spelled out in sign language the bickering going on to Jim's amusement.

It was a good thing that they were all able to get together in such a way, as it was good for the entire class to have the opportunity to begin to address such questions as: who were they, what were they called to do, and where were they called to go.

The opening session introduced the subject of general expectations held by those entering seminary—the very same subject Bob, David, and John had discussed on the grounds of the Washington Monument on their first weekend together. It was no surprise to them, therefore, that people had come to seminary for different reasons—some personal, some religious, and some social in nature. Some had come because they were certain they wanted to be priests, but some came to evade the army draft. Some were called to social activism and some to churchmanship. Some were merely searching for life's meaning. Although some felt whole, some felt lost, alone, and afraid. But as discussion sessions would reveal on Saturday, confusion, doubt, lack of understanding, and the pain of not knowing either the will of God or maybe even God Himself compounded those reasons.

All of those issues seeped out at Roslyn to be wrestled with and aired. Because of previous discussions along those same lines with former classes and from personal knowledge as well, the members of the faculty were no strangers to the experiences and feelings being shared. So in the midst of not having all of the answers to all of the questions, the instructors could still offer what was considered to be a good theological education, along with faith, hope, love, and prayer that by the grace of God the pieces of the puzzle would ultimately fit together.

Thus, a level of trust began to develop between the students and their teachers, as well as among the students themselves as barriers came tumbling down. It was an interesting time and a frightening one as well, for after all, from just those sorts and conditions of people was supposed to emerge the future leadership of the Episcopal Church.

"If so," they thought, "God help us."

After returning to VTS, participants continued to ponder their experience in Roslyn in different ways. Bob, David, and John felt reassured that they were not alone in questioning what lay ahead. In fact, the weekend gave them more certainty than ever about the direction in which they were heading.

The scary thing was that if they and their classmates were the ones who were going to be defending the faith in the future, where could the church possibly be heading? What happened to the men and women of strong belief cited in the Bible? Or was it that those ancient heroes doubted, complained, asked questions, felt confused, and found God to be just as remote as modern people—even theological students—sometimes did? Maybe all that stuff about the Israelites murmuring and wandering in the wilderness was beginning to make sense. God had waited forty years to deliver them to His promised land. But the message seemed to be getting clearer and clearer to at least a few members of the junior class that even though God was never in a hurry, He was always on time.

So even in their confusion and misunderstanding, still there was something the junior class could both hold onto and proclaim. It also seemed to be clearer and clearer that Holy Scripture was not so much a record of absolute truth as it was a record of belief and faith, discovery and proclamation—all in the very face of doubt and adversity.

Thus it was that all those thoughts came to the forefront as four seminarians sat at a small table in a little bar across from the Uptown Cinerama Theater in Washington, DC. It was the same Saturday they had returned from the conference but much later in the afternoon. All agreed that the retreat was too intense an experience to process quickly, but since Ed had driven his car with others aboard to and from Roslyn, he was now playing catch up with his three colleagues about what they all felt had taken place.

Having reached the saturation point in their weighty discussion, they walked across the street to where *2001: A Space Odyssey*, one of the most thought-provoking films of the year, was playing. Instead of finding the relaxation they hoped for during the next three hours, the Wilmerites found themselves merely channeling their agitated mental energy in a different direction. Still the change of focus was a good diversion, and they returned to Wilmer Hall exhausted.

The feature was to cause a great deal of discussion over the days and weeks to come as the four of them analyzed the philosophical and theological aspects of the cinematic saga. But by the time they got to their rooms that evening, there was only enough energy left to say good night.

Science fiction was still in vogue at the beginning of the next week as Bob, David, and John gathered in Ed's room for the afternoon color presentation of the 1951 film classic *When Worlds Collide.* Unfortunately, as was often the case with television matinées, some scenes were cut and replaced by commercials so that the showing could fit into a neat block of time. Still it was an enjoyable way to return to the routine of classes after the intense weekend that had just passed.

Looking ahead, Bob, John, and Ed were aware of the fact that on Thursday, October 10th, David would celebrate his twenty-second birthday, so behind his back they planned a surprise party. But even before festivities took place, the evening already brimmed with frivolity.

After supper Bob, David, and Roy heard a fellow class-mate playing an old gospel hymn in Scott Lounge, which drew them in like flies to honey. Bob eagerly joined in on "Amazing Grace," and with his perfect pitch, delighted and horrified the others with his amazing ability to drag out a note and slide into the next one with the same overall effect of dragging one's fingernails across a chalkboard. It was the most deliberately awful off-key version of a hymn that anyone had ever heard and enough to make one's skin crawl.

The impromptu songfest continued to draw in other

singers, but after a while the limited repertoire of the pianist became a little monotonous. When efforts to dislodge him from his perch bore no fruit, David remembered something that had happened in college. With Patty and two friends, he had been riding behind the driver in the backseat of a Volkswagen with his hand resting all the way through the passenger assist strap. The driver noticed that the stylized way David's fingers touched his thumb looked just like a duck. The duck promptly pinched the driver's nose.

Remembering that incident, David thought he might try a similar move in the present situation to see what kind of reaction he would get. Transforming his hand into a duck once again, he began to lightly pinch the pianist's ear, and everyone began to snicker.

That story quickly spread around campus, so that later Don Wimberly caused a chuckle when he inquired of Bob, John, and Ed, "Where's the duck?" The man from Tennessee was thus to be tagged with a nickname that remained with him for the rest of his life.

By the time "the Duck" returned to Wilmer Hall that evening, he had become increasingly concerned that something was going on behind his back. Conversations and whisperings had continued for the previous few days. All during the communion service that evening, he feared that somehow he had done or said something wrong that perhaps ran the risk of his being excluded from the new community he so deeply cherished. He had known that feeling of exclusion in the past when growing up, and he prayed to God that it was not happening again.

A short time after they all returned to the dorm, Ed burst out of his room next door, yelling that his waste paper basket was on fire. Drawn to the flickering light that David could see through the crack in the door, he ran into Ed's room to find twenty-two birthday candles burning brightly. His three friends began to sing "Happy Birthday," led by Bob in all of his radiant tenor voice—that time fortunately on key. As David listened with moist eyes, he silently thanked his God for the friends surrounding him.

"Thank you," he said aloud as the song ended. "I've been scared to death over the past few days that something I'd said or done had caused some gap between us. Needless to say, I'm thankful it has not. But worrying about it has helped me realize once again how much you guys mean to me. So in more ways than one, this party means more than you could know."

The room grew quiet. Bob, John, and Ed had not expected an emotional response. But it made them realize too, that their friendship was a special one indeed. Then, with the pop of a champagne cork amid cheers, handshakes, and hugs, the friends savored the tender sweetness of a birthday cake.

As the party broke up, David thought Roy might like a piece of the action, so he took a slice of cake over to his room in St. George's Hall. Roy was glad to see him and received his treat gratefully. Then he broke out into a laugh when he noticed that David had written on the napkin beneath the cake, "Happy Birthday to me!" and signed it, "The Duck."

A couple of weeks later, David wrote his latest epistle to Patty. As usual, he reviewed the events that had transpired since he last had talked to her on the hallway phone. Much was happening within and without the halls of VTS. The launch of the first Apollo mission and the marriage of Jackie Kennedy to Aristotle Onassis had been in the news, and the seminarians had just completed their mid-term examinations. David also reported on the Wilmerites' day trip to Mount Vernon, as well as the poignant viewing with Jim Alby of the film version of *The Heart Is a Lonely Hunter*,

Carson McCullers' drama about a deaf mute.

David also recounted how he and John had enjoyed watching a matinée presentation of *The High and the Mighty* on television. Shortened, of course, by the need for commercial breaks, it was still one of their all time favorites.

Wrapping up his letter to Patty, David asked her what was happening in her life, and then having already told her the story of his new nickname, he closed in anticipation of seeing her in about a month. With an expression of his love, he ended with one final word: "Quack!"

CHAPTER 7

Northern breezes scattered russet and gold leaves across the quadrangle. With midterms completed, the rest of the quarter was proceeding quietly. The big news on the national scene was the presidential election on November 5th, won by Richard Nixon and his campaign to restore order to the many American cities that had erupted in violence and protest after the murder of Martin Luther King Jr.

From campus the out-of-state seminarians sent in their absentee ballots, and as the day of decision drew near, everyone was anxious to see who would be chosen. The popular vote between the two main candidates wound up being extremely close, and the whole process created an interesting diversion from academic life.

Politics were also playing themselves out at VTS, for by that time the juniors had elected their class officers and representatives for the student body association. The central characters of this story had been either so engrossed in the extracurricular activities of the college scene or so removed from it that the politics of campus life did not seem to interest them at all. They were quite content to let the more issues-minded people run the various aspects of student government.

It was time to decide where clinical training would take place the following summer. As the seminarians received letters from their bishops suggesting places they might consider, they began meeting with campus representatives of the various programs. Then came the applications to be filled out, the biographies to compose, the pictures made, and final placement conferences.

One good thing that came out of all this for David was deepening his relationship with his married colleagues who hailed from Tennessee—Robert Sessum and Carl Cunningham. Even though Carl's freckles refuted his age, he was actually more than ten years older, but David still considered him to be both friend and peer. They both looked up to Robert who was a class year ahead of them. Thanks to their bishop's recommendation of the Memphis Institute of Medicine and Religion, Carl and David spent some enjoyable hours together discussing the same place where Robert had done his clinical training, a site that both Carl and David already were favorably considering. Carl ultimately decided to go elsewhere; David choose to follow Robert's lead and head to western Tennessee the following June.

In addition to choosing clinical training sites, the time was not that far distant when field work placements would be determined. Members of the junior class continued to visit various nearby churches where they might get the practical experience of parish work during their second and third years. Although final decisions did not have to be made until after the first of the year, with so many choices available, they needed time to investigate their options.

Since having made their trip to Grace Church in Alexandria on their first Sunday at seminary, Bob, David, and John had visited several other churches. One of the most memorable was St. Paul's on K Street in Washington. Of all the high churches in the land, that one seemed to have taken the cake. Fifteen minutes into the service, you could hardly see the altar because of the smoking incense. Even Bob, who loved every minute of an Anglo-Catholic service, began to cough a bit.

As they headed out of the smog toward the car following worship, Bob began to chuckle about a churchman he had known who had grown up believing that a worship service was just not valid without an offering of incense. That "high church" friend had gone on to attend Virginia Theological Seminary, which was known for its much more informal style of liturgical expression. Upon graduation, he had the opportunity to serve as a thurifer once more. But that time as he swung the smoking thurible toward the congregants, he realized that incense was not the vital means to enter the presence of God that he had once believed it to be. "Incense," he thought, "don't do no good; don't do no harm."

The Wilmerites also ventured across the color barrier to St. Mary's on 23rd Street in the District of Columbia. Before, during, and after the service, that small congregation made the white visitors feel not different but welcome as fellow pilgrims in every way, practicing their Christian faith together. Afterward, Bob and John smiled in agreement when David commented: "The communion wine tasted just the same."

The three joined Ed one Sunday to attend Church of the Redeemer in Baltimore—Ed's old parish where he had previously worked as an acolyte trainer and hoped to work again. But the parishes that attracted the other three were St. Andrew's and St. George's in Arlington, and St. Francis in Potomac, Maryland.

Bob felt that St. Andrew's in Arlington came the closest to meeting his needs. The rector, also named Andrews, manifested the style of ministry and worship in his churchmanship from which Bob felt he could best learn.

Not far from where Bob would be working, David picked St. George's in Arlington because it had been recommended by both the seminarians presently serving there and by the director of field education. As he had professed earlier, the man from Tennessee had absolutely no idea whether or not he even wanted to be involved in parish ministry, but that was perfectly all right with the rector, Father Hedley Williams, who was willing to let him go and grow at his own pace.

John was locked into St. Francis in Potomac, Maryland because he had enjoyed working before with the rector, the Reverend Ed Sims, and wanted to do so again.

Once clinical training and field education plans jelled, the remainder of their first quarter seemed to slow down considerably. With the fresh novelty of seminary life behind them, classes settled into a sometimes-monotonous routine. But there was an issue surfacing that had begun to separate the junior class into two distinct groups.

The married and single students were starting to drift apart. Not that they really had been that close before, but since the retreat at Roslyn, it was becoming evident that class members were experiencing one of two entirely different lifestyles, each with its own set of pros and cons.

Basically, the married men got up in the morning and "went to work," coming home in the afternoon to their wives and children. Though they were in school, it was the same sort of routine that they had experienced before coming to seminary and would continue after graduating. But nightly homework assignments limited family interaction. Even when there was time to spend together, it seemed that husbands and wives did not have all that much in common because of their different daily schedules. And because they were married, interaction with others—even other married seminarians—was limited at best.

On the other hand, the single students had more opportunities to discuss with their fellow residents all that was
going on. Late night conversations were known to last until
3:00 or 4:00 in the morning. Obviously a real sense of community was developing on the campus in both small and
large circles, and everyone who participated was benefiting
both spiritually and intellectually.

The disadvantage for the single students was the challenge of finding any kind of break from routine on the
holy hill. Roy dated a few of the women on campus. Jim
taught sign language to anyone interested. Ed enjoyed
smoking his cigarettes and watching his color television.
John loved to read and study in his methodical manner.
Bob listened to his records incessantly and played bridge
with Henry Witten. And "Duck," as David was being called
more and more, slipped away to a movie whenever he
could—always with a bag of popcorn and a cold Coca-
Cola in hand.

All in all, the worlds of the married and the single existed
alongside one another like parallel universes. Only once in
a while did something happen to bring them all together.
Probably nothing did so like the announcement that was
made on Tuesday, November 12th.

Molle had told his morning class that if they chose not
to go to the later forum hour, each and every one of them
would probably regret it for the rest of their lives. Everyone,
of course, attended, and they didn't have to wait long before
learning the shocking news that was to shape all who were
present—their time there, their years to come, and the very
future of the seminary.

Dean Trotter was resigning.

A few days later, after the initial impact of the announcement had worn off, Bob finished another letter home. It
was the first really long one that he had written his mother
since he arrived at VTS. The longer epistle offered him for
the first time a chance to let his hair down and talk about
himself, his beliefs, his life, and his seminary.

As Jim had already discovered in borrowing his class
notes, Bob was one of the most thorough, complete, fluent,
and eloquent writers that had graced the Virginia campus
in a long time. So it was no particular surprise that Bob's
composition to his mother captured the profound effect
that had been made on the academic community almost
as well, if not better, than the letters, resolutions, state-
ments, speeches, and declarations that had followed the
resignation of Jesse Trotter as dean. However, there was
one article from a seminary journal on which he felt he
could not personally improve, so he repeated it verbatim
to his mother in order to capture the essence of the man
in question:

> And so thirteen years of a man's life in one field
> has come to a close. It is perhaps at such deaths in
> one's life, like that final time of death, that we look
> back at his entire career to see just what he has and
> has not done. Jesse Trotter is a man who has done
> and indeed has done well.
>
> He was born in Chattanooga, Tennessee, and
> graduated from VTS in 1936, having served as the
> president of the student body his senior year. In

1939 he married Marion, and in 1946 he was called here as Associate Professor of Apologetics, the same year that married students had their advent on campus. He was elected Dean in 1956, and to say that he accomplished much in his tenure would be a gross understatement.

Interestingly enough, his very desire to yield the position of administrative head was based on his belief that he had accomplished what he set out to do: a new curriculum, additional programs and personnel to carry them out, faculty housing on the campus, and the successful completion of a seven and one half million dollar development program. But all of those reasons were not the only ones why he wanted to resign as Dean. He desired to return to teaching because he saw the student body in the present era in a crisis of belief, and he felt that he needed to offer the remaining years of his ministry as a gift of his time, his attention, and his friendship to the students of tomorrow.

Bob paused for a moment. Not that there was nothing left to say, but perhaps that was sufficient for his mom for now. After all, the rest of the story really lay in the future. So he closed his letter with love.

The board of trustees appointed a committee to plan the transition from one dean to the next. Perhaps as appropriate a move as that was, students and faculty both were aware of the humorous irony of that action, knowing Molle's famous line about group decisions: "For God so loved the world that He did not send a committee."

When the board did meet to appoint that nine-member committee—one of whom was to be a student—two other important decisions were also made: first, to build a gymnasium named after Dr. Mollegen, and second, to build a continuing education building adjacent to Wilmer Hall.

The latter action met with an initially negative response from the single members of the student body because they had enjoyed the presence of the men from the field who stayed in their dorms for six weeks while there for reflection. The chance to interact with them had been beneficial on many levels, and relegating the elders to their own quarters seemed to be a step backward. Plus, for the Wilmerites, that change meant the loss of their convenient parking circle. However, in understanding that the one constant in life was change, everyone moved forward together, once again acknowledging the valuable contribution that Jesse Trotter had made to the life of the Virginia Theological Seminary.

His legacy would be a tremendous one. He was a profound man, rooted firmly in the Bible, and his ministry centered in service to Jesus Christ. Even in the midst of personal tragedy in his own life when he suffered the loss of a son to suicide, he could still respond in faith: "I have been to the bottom and found it firm."

CHAPTER 8

And so it was with all the aforementioned events on their minds that the seminary community sailed toward the end of the first quarter. Finals were upon them sooner than they realized, and wandering thoughts about what their ministries might look like in the future intertwined with their studies.

Thanksgiving called most of the seminarians home, but Bob and John decided to remain on campus for the short holiday hiatus. Nothing could keep David from seeing Patty. They had arranged for him to meet her in Roanoke so they could drive home together to Chattanooga. David looked forward to the break. He both needed and wanted time to return to familiar surroundings, to acknowledge his transition from the past to the present, and to affirm that what had been important to him before was still important to him.

The trip turned out to be a good one, complemented by the fact that his grades for the first quarter had averaged about like his college classes had. David was more or less a "B" student, as was Bob. Of our three primary characters, there had never been any question that John was the scholar of the group. Suffice it to say, the first quarter grades surprised no one.

After the break, David had met Jim in Roanoke, staying with him and some friends over a Saturday night and trying to communicate the best he could in sign language; then beginning the new church year the next morning at St. John's Episcopal Church downtown, they arrived back on campus around dinner time, excited to reunite with Bob and John. All of them were ready to strengthen a friendship clearly of a lasting nature. John suggested that since they had no homework that night, they should start off the new term properly by visiting a place that had recently become one of their favorite haunts, Hot Shoppes.

As they ate their burgers, the men of Wilmer anticipated taking up their studies once more. The second quarter would see the substitution of pastoral theology for systematic theology, but other than that change, the rest of the schedule simply advanced the same courses they had already taken to the next level. Other than a Tuesday afternoon speech class, the juniors would still find themselves seated in Aspinwall Hall in the mornings for lectures with afternoons free to study or amuse themselves.

Of course, there were some faculty shifts in the classrooms. They lamented that Molle was on sabbatical leave for the rest of the year. As has already been noted, he had made a profound effect on the newest members of the student body—not the least of which was having taken over an ill Dr. Reid's New Testament survey course for the remainder of the term. Though he did a wonderful job, humorously enough the good doctor came into class on the last day of the quarter, having just realized that the school was no longer on the semester system. So, in seventy-five minutes, he completed the overview of the synoptic gospels by finishing Mark, covering Matthew and Luke, reconstructing the historical Jesus, and still leaving time for questions.

Fortunately, a hale and hearty Dr. Reid returned to the mix, for which everyone was thankful. There were some advisor shifts too. David was pleased to find himself assigned to Dean Trotter, since Dr. Rogers was also on sabbatical leave. Bob and John stayed on with Dr. Allison and Dr. Graham respectively. David and Roy would continue the study of Greek, with Bob and John choosing other electives, only to discover other endearing faculty members like Dr. Clifford Stanley. Thus they were off and running for the second quarter.

Having found dinner in the refectory not particularly appetizing one evening, David and John decided to venture back to Chuck's Carry-Out for pizza, that time to order it with everything, including anchovies, which David fondly remembered having embellished a pizza he had enjoyed a while back in Chattanooga. The problem was that this pie was insufficiently cooked, and while John drove the two of them back to the dorm, David noticed that the contents of the box sitting on his lap were leaking onto his pants. When they got back to Wilmer Hall, David dashed off to change his trousers while John carried the pizza into the common room.

Opening it up, he discovered that all of the anchovies had been dumped in the center of the pie instead of being strewn over it. David returned, and he and John made it through two bites before they decided their acquisition reeked so strongly that it simply had to be tossed. To prevent the odor from lingering over the dorm, they dumped it in an outside trash can and chalked up the experience as a lost cause. However, it not only took hours for the smell to leave the common room, but David eventually had to throw away his trousers because no amount of washing would eradicate the fishy scent. Needless to say they never, ever returned to Chuck's Carry-Out. In fact, for a couple of weeks around the campus there was a running joke that two dogs and a cat had discovered the pizza in the trash can. Consuming it, the two dogs had died instantly, and the cat had last been seen carrying a sign that read, "Unclean! Unclean!"

Only three weeks separated the Thanksgiving and Christmas breaks. And having endured the sleepless nights as the junior class studied for their first finals, then taking a week off for Thanksgiving, it was hard to get going again, especially knowing that in just twenty-one days things would once again come to a halt until the new year arrived. So, the three-week interim really was just that, an interlude without a great deal of study undertaken.

The gap was seen as more of an introductory session to the second quarter, a time when everybody became familiar with what they were going to study but lived in almost a holding pattern until after the first of the year when they would get back down to business. The Old Testament course was to center on the time of Samuel, while the New Testament class was to focus on the Acts of the Apostles. Dr. Newman gave one of his famous content quizzes before the break, but other than that, no one laid their shoulder to the wheel. And even for that test, there was certainly not as much work put into it as there had been for the first one, and certainly not as much as they had devoted to the professor's final exam.

It was clear that the student body was looking forward to Christmas. David wrote Patty and asked her if she would join him in Roanoke to then drive home together, so he was looking forward to being with his girl again. John was preparing to fly home; Bob was going to drive all the way to Texas.

After only twelve of the twenty-one days slated to be back on campus, however, the dean discontinued classes when a flu epidemic broke out in Washington and its environs. Though Dr. Trotter's intentions were good and potentially preventative, still about one-half of the seminary community came down with the "bug" anyway. Ultimately administration decided to start the Christmas break a week ahead of schedule, since it seemed better to send fifty percent of the people home sick early rather than to wait and perhaps send everyone home sick on time.

The early release came as an odd disappointment to some because those who were well had begun a special type of ministry to those who were afflicted. Bob, David, and John had managed to avoid the contamination, but Ed and Roy were affected. All over campus, the able-bodied took on the servant nature of Jesus as they carried sick trays back and forth to dorm rooms, ran errands, and checked on how the sick were faring. It was not the way they had planned to celebrate the Lord's birth, but they experienced the presence of Christ in their midst all the same. All were beginning to realize they were loved not only by God but more and more by one another and that they were not alone.

All in all, the seminary community came closer together during that experience, as they had in their common concern over whom the new dean might be and how the country would fare once President Nixon was inaugurated. Although necessary, it was difficult for them to part company at such a time, but so they did.

It had been a profound year, 1968. So many different things had happened in so many different ways. New beginnings had been made, ones that would never be duplicated.

All were to arrive safely at their destinations. All would enjoy the holidays. All would anticipate their return to a new life preparing for the ministry. Somehow they each knew and felt to be true what had been mentioned to them one Thursday night in a sermon—that each day would be the first day of the rest of their lives. They would look forward to sharing as many of them as possible together.

CHAPTER 9

The year 1969, like all years, began with the promise of new life, with a chance to start over—to do things that had not been done before and to stop doing all those things that should have been stopped long ago. And for a select group of people, 1969 would be a year to renew the acquaintances and relationships that had been interrupted by a flu epidemic.

That had been only three and a half weeks prior, but it seemed like much longer, for the development of their new life together had been cut short, and they were anxious to pick up where they left off. So once more, members of a seminary community came together from places far and near to begin again and to share their lives anew.

In a way the previous four months had been a prelude to all that was to come in the two and a half years that lay ahead. Those would be years that would run the gamut of emotions and experiences, time that would offer opportunities to experience both life and death, renewal and resurrection, ministry and service—all on the path to the priesthood. Though none of the students knew exactly how that path would unfold, they were eager to commence.

David reflected on all of those things as he drove the road to Roanoke. He was without Patty that time, she being busy back in Chattanooga making plans for her own future in

X-ray technology. With the Holiday Inn full, David checked into a Travel Lodge, happy to find it with both a color television and the lower rate of ten dollars a night instead of twelve. After taking in a film, then enjoying a long shower, he plopped onto the bed with a take-out hamburger, watched a few programs, and drifted off to sleep.

After resting well and downing a big breakfast, the Tennessean hit the road again to travel the four hours to Alexandria. It had hit him that the rest stop in Roanoke was a bit of a paradox because in either direction he traveled, he felt he was heading home.

John returned first to the Virginia campus, having arrived by air. He was busy washing and waxing his car when Bob drove in from Texas, smoke-free. Having decided over the break that he would give up smoking, he did just that, never to return to it.

Bob had, however, brought an alternate diversion. Pets were not permitted really, but no one would be complaining about Jigger, the parakeet who was immediately adopted as the dorm mascot. Jigger was friendly and even sported a few tricks to entertain visitors to Bob's room. If one were to hold out both arms, one hand touching the mirror over the sink, Jigger would fly to land on the opposite hand, walk up that arm, across the shoulders, and down the other arm, to admire himself in the mirror.

As another extracurricular activity that quarter, David bought from Bruce Myers a tape recorder so that he could make cassettes of his favorite music. Bruce had also been instrumental in getting the residents of the dorm together each day for a glass or two of sherry in his room. Everyone looked forward to the five-o'clock social hour before dinner, and one of the more memorable stories that occurred on the holy hill happened during one of those gatherings. Bob loved to read, especially in the late afternoon. Often, he enjoyed a glass of sherry with his dorm mates, then took a second one back to his room to sip while he continued to peruse his books and periodicals. Jigger became used to the routine, and since Bob left the cage door open, the bird often flew out, perched on the edge of the sherry glass, and dipped in his beak for a sip or two. Sometimes, the parakeet was even known to get a little tipsy.

One day, however, Bob decided to have an afternoon cup of coffee instead. Thinking the routine was the same, Jigger flew out of his cage, perched on the cup rim, and dipped his beak into the hot liquid. Out came a screech, followed by a cloud of feathers zooming out the door and down the hallway. Jigger bounced off the screen door at the entrance and landed in a soft pile on the floor. The bird was not hurt but seemed a bit embarrassed.

Thus with the presence now of a small feathered friend, life moved on. January 9th brought the first opportunity to order ecclesiastical vestments. Given his Anglo-Catholic background, Bob was the most excited about ordering his first set of basic garments—a cassock and surplice. He wanted to make sure that he ordered the best garments from the best company at the best price, and it came to $42 for the set. He was able to secure them in a wash-and-wear material, which was comfortable yet durable. John and David followed his lead.

When field education placements were issued, each one of our central characters was pleased to find that he got his first choice, which included an interesting coincidence: Father Andrews, who appropriately led St. Andrew's Church where Bob was to serve, had entered the ministry later in life and had served his assistantship at St. George's under Father Williams, where David was to serve.

In addition to study, social activities continued. David and John toured the Washington Monument on Friday, January 17th, and on Saturday Bob and David drove to the MacArthur Theater outside of Georgetown to see the motion picture version of the musical *Oliver!* Both of them came back raving about it. John took the recommendation of David, the film buff, more seriously that Bob's. The Texan had a tendency to exaggerate the superior quality of any given particular—person, place, or thing.

Ed summed it up well by saying: "Bob, the best thing about you is that you've never met any mediocre people."

Clinical training assignments soon came in, and David was pleased to see that he had been accepted in Memphis. The term was to last from June 9th to August 28th, so he immediately began to think about what vacation time with Patty he could squeeze in around the edges.

President Nixon was inaugurated on Monday, January 20th, and everyone huddled around television sets to witness the historic event. On the 23rd, a meeting of the entire student body was held to gather information from the class members as to their criteria for a new dean. Bob felt that it was not the students' place to be a part of the decision-making process, but the board of trustees had already decided to solicit community input.

The priests-to-be asked questions, voiced their opinions, and shared their thoughts. All in all, another opportunity had presented itself for all to grow closer to one another, to broaden understanding of different mindsets, and to have a say in the planning of what would be a new chapter in the history of the school.

Everyone was honored to begin to live into the future of the seminary.

Something was missing. "Duck" couldn't quite figure out what it was, but something was still not quite right about his room. The green area rug had added some needed color, but something was missing.

One night, instead of sleeping he stared at the remaining blank wall in his room. A built-in chest of drawers stood next to a mirror over a sink, which stood next to a closet. What could a decorator do with that? Then it hit him.

With a free period the next morning, David dashed off to purchase a green shower curtain, rod, and hardware. Stringing the curtain over the open closet and the recessed lavatory worked perfectly. It allowed him easy access to either washing or dressing areas, yet screened each from view when not in use. Plus, the color complemented the rug. John liked the idea so much he later adorned his room with a shower curtain of his own.

On David's way to lunch he ran into his fellow Tennessee colleagues, Carl Cunningham and Robert Sessum, and that offered the threesome a chance to discuss an interesting rumor that Robert had heard. Their bishop was expected soon for his annual visitation.

"Just as long as he doesn't come this Sunday night, I don't care when he arrives," David said. "Several of us have tickets for Peter, Paul, and Mary, and I don't want to miss that concert."

"You just wait and see," Robert said. "He'll probably be in this afternoon, and you'll have some useless tickets on your hands."

"No chance," David replied.

Carl laughed at the interchange between his friends, but wondered along with them just when the prelate might arrive. After all, they had been in Virginia long enough now, and each one of them was looking forward to sharing experiences with their chief pastor, as well as speculating about what their future might hold.

David left the table, still vowing not to give up his tickets, and headed back to his room. There he found a note on his door, which read: "Bishop Vander Horst is in Moore Hall and would like an appointment with you this afternoon."

"Sessum, you fox," David muttered under his breath, and hurried out of the dorm and back to the refectory to assure his colleague that the practical joke had not worked.

It never occurred to him that the message might be authentic, nor did he wonder how Robert could have gotten the note on his door so quickly after lunch. But then he really did not have all that much time to think about it, for as David headed back into the dining area, he came face to face with the Right Reverend John Vander Horst himself.

"Well, Mr. Chamberlain, I believe," the short, stocky bishop uttered.

The youngest postulant for Holy Orders from the Diocese of Tennessee stood there in dismay. Somehow he managed to utter a few words of welcome and even joke about how nice it had been to have advance warning of his visit; then when asked when they could have the proposed appointment, he suggested that right then was as good a time as any. So, after a quick visit to Wilmer Hall for presentation of his home on the hill, David and his future boss retired to the guest quarters.

"What do you think about all of this?" Patty's former rector of St. Paul's, Chattanooga, posed in his gravelly voice. David thought to himself that if the bishop's life had ever been portrayed on film, James Cagney would have been the perfect one to play the part.

David then gave a short dissertation on how interesting graduate school for the ministry was proving to be, how important friends and faculty were becoming, and how thankful the Tennesseans were to be there.

"Speaking of being thankful, how's your spiritual life?" Bishop Jack uttered. "It can get lost at this place, David. You know I was here, and I don't think there's another place like Virginia, but watch your spiritual life."

The conversation continued for a good hour or so. Both had a chance to talk, to share, and to get to know one another better. Then, with a slap of his knee, the prelate announced that Chamberlain was taken care of for the time being. The conversation concluded with questions about how Carl and Robert were doing. David had to laugh, explaining the discourse that had taken place at lunch and the unusual circumstances that had caused him to return to the refectory. The bishop laughed as well, then handing him the phone numbers asked David if he would be so kind as to call the other two, include their spouses, and arrange a place and time for him to treat them all to dinner. While Vander Horst unpacked, David picked up the phone and dialed.

Carl was easy to contact, though suspicious at first that he also might be the victim of a hoax. Grabbing the phone from David, the purple-clad cleric bellowed into the mouth-piece, "Cunningham, what time are you picking me up for dinner?"

With the bishop having cleared up any question of his presence, the two classmates began to discuss the local restaurant scene while the bishop whistled merrily in the background. Carl remembered Robert saying at lunch that

the best place they could go when the diocesan came was
The Three Thieves in Washington.

"Fine," the prelate said, and Carl and David smiled, knowing they were in for a good meal.

The Cunninghams agreed that they would try to get in
touch with the Sessums and provide transportation for the
evening; all would meet at the bishop's room at six o'clock.

David then returned to his room. He had hoped to have
the afternoon free, because among other things, that Friday
was the beginning of the college conference on the ministry for singles. Men from all over the country were invited
to come for a weekend to find out just what seminary life
was like. The visitors were to room with some of the single
students, and David was one of those who had offered
accommodations.

Fortunately, so had Bob and John, who having met
David's bishop, understood the situation, and were happy
to entertain Duck's guest until he returned from dinner.

David prepared for his first trip to The Three Thieves
and walked to Moore Hall. It was about 5:45 p.m. when he
arrived at his bishop's door. They had a few minutes of casual
conversation before Nelia and Carl arrived. Vander Horst
greeted them with a warm two-word welcome:

"Where's Sessum?"

"Hello, sir, nice to see you too," the Cunninghams replied.
"We hate to tell you, but we were never able to reach either
Donna or Robert."

"I'll get Sessum for this," his Grace retorted.

Nelia started to say something, but Carl stopped her,
thinking that was neither the time nor the place for comment. All in all, they had a fun evening at the restaurant,
decorated to look like a medieval castle. After consuming
a round of drinks, the younger diners tried to contain their

grins as the waitress draped the prelate with a lobster bib.

"I wish I had a camera," David said.

"Shut up, or I'll claw you," the diocesan warned.

That remark drew a groan from the other three as they all dove into a hearty meal. When the waitress brought the bill, Bishop Jack took one look at it, crossed himself, and moaned. He ribbed his fellow diners for having the audacity to read the menu from the left side of the page, where the names of the dishes were printed, rather than from the more important right side of the page, where the prices were listed. The senior cleric was easily appeased, however, when he was offered and accepted an invitation for all of them to return to the Cunninghams' for after-dinner drinks.

Later, as they were sipping their cordials, the prelate asked David to try calling the Sessums one more time, which he agreed to do even though it was close to 9:30 p.m.

"Hello," a distracted male voice answered.

"Robert, this is David Chamberlain. You're not going to believe what I'm about to tell you."

"OK, so tell me," replied the voice.

"I'm at the Cunninghams' place," said David, "and guess who is here with us?"

"I don't believe it, Chamberlain; you're just pulling my leg."

"Robert, I'm telling you, the bishop is here at Carl and Nelia's right now. I am not lying."

"Don't give me that stuff, Chamberlain," said the voice with rising irritation.

"Robert, I am not kidding."

Carl walked over and asked David to hand him the phone.

"Hey, buddy," said Carl. "Listen, you better get your ass over here, because THE MAN is here. We are not fooling."

"I just don't buy any of this," Robert persisted.

The bishop grabbed the phone from Carl.

"Sessum," the cleric's voice raged over the wire. "Get over here now! . . . Sessum, are you there?"

Fifteen minutes later the doorbell rang, and in walked Donna and Robert.

"Well, that's the first time I've ever had a bishop interrupt my sex life," Robert announced.

"That's a fine thing to say," said Vander Horst. "Where have you two been? Don't you know when I come to town, everything is supposed to stop while you all jump?"

"But . . ." Robert tried to interrupt.

"Don't you 'but' me. Why I ought to pack you all up and ship you back to Memphis."

The diocesan was having a grand time tearing the Sessums down, and Robert and Donna had been around Vander Horst long enough to understand his trademark humor. Carl and David just eyed each other while all that was going on, but Nelia was not quite sure whether what was happening was fact or fiction. At any rate, she'd had enough. She had reached the boiling point over the whole evening, and she was about to go on the warpath.

"Bishop, I've got something to say. I am damn tired of listening to you bitch at the Sessums. I don't care whether you're the bishop or the pope. You're in my house, all of you are my guests, and I'm tired of listening to this trash. If you had an ounce of social grace or decency, you would have let us know a long time ago about your plans to be here, and that would have solved the whole problem. Donna and Robert would have been able to be part of the dinner, instead of part of this tirade, which is really your fault anyway. It's just lucky none of the rest of us were tied up for the evening.

"Maybe it would have been better if we had been. Maybe it would have taught you some manners. So from now on, you might try treating your seminarians like human beings, with enough respect to get in touch with us ahead of time. But whatever you do, you can just stop talking about it tonight. I'm tired. The Sessums have or had other things on their minds. And if you don't like it, why don't you leave town and come back when you can deal with us in a more mature fashion?

"Now I've had my piece. You can kick us out too if you like. I'm sure we can survive. But as long as you're in my house, you can keep quiet about the Sessums."

Needless to say, a long pause followed. In fact, it seemed eternal. David sat with his eyes closed, not knowing what to expect next. Robert and Carl stared at each other, and Donna stared at the wall. Finally, the bishop looked at Nelia.

"Are you quite finished, Mrs. Cunningham?"

"Yes," Nelia affirmed.

"Thank you," the prelate uttered. "I have been well reprimanded."

As unbelievable as it seemed, the Right Revered John Vander Horst had been silenced. For a brief moment, everyone thought that either the bishop might do something terrible or that, at the least, he had been offended. Probably, he once again was made aware of the fact that not everyone appreciated his particular style of humor, and perhaps that he needed to win back the affection of Mrs. Cunningham.

Actually, his apology had done that already. Before the night was over, they all were laughing about the whole thing. Bishop Jack still managed to get in a few wise cracks, but never without physically ducking from Nelia's glare, which both angered and amused her all at the same time. Robert's main complaint remained that his sex life had been interrupted.

Back in Wilmer Hall David got a kick out of telling the story to his dorm mates and the single visitors. They enjoyed it too, as well as being both amazed and amused that a bishop of the church could be stood up to like that.

The experience was a meaningful one for all. David reflected on it with Bob as they watched a late night science-fiction movie on the small television set he had brought back from Texas.

"Maybe part of the gift of this evening was that you got to see your bishop as a human being, with both his strengths and his weaknesses," Bob offered.

"You're probably right," David replied. "I think often we place our senior pastors on too high a pedestal. Not that we shouldn't look up to them with respect, but I guess when you see that purple attire, you feel intimidated. Because of tonight, I don't think I'll feel that way anymore."

So, the first seminary encounter with his bishop had come to pass, one that David knew he would remember for a long time to come, and one that would continue to play a meaningful part in his life in many ways.

One of those ways manifested that very weekend before the college conference on the ministry was concluded The young man who had roomed with David expressed his appreciation not only for the hospitality, but also for the opportunity to see that not only seminarians but also bishops were just people—people who did not have everything together, people who were still works in progress. More than anything else, that awareness had made him more comfortable about taking his own next step toward the ministry.

The single visitors departed as Sunday evening arrived. Normally, the Wilmerites would have gathered in Ed's room to watch *Mission: Impossible* in color. But that night, February 9th, Peter, Paul, and Mary were playing at the DAR

Constitution Hall in downtown DC. Thankfully the concert had not conflicted with a particular bishop's schedule. So, with Bob otherwise committed, there they sat—John, Ed, and David—on the very front row. It was as special an event as they could have hoped for.

All of the folk trio's music was special, but there were two songs that stood out for David. One was called "The First Time Ever I Saw Your Face," which reminded him of Patty and how much he would miss being with her on St. Valentine's Day. At least it wouldn't be long until he saw her again. The other song was entitled "Bob Dylan's Dream," which reminded all of them just how special and important friendships were—and just how thankful they were to be together at VTS.

All in all, it had turned out to be a most eventful and meaningful weekend.

CHAPTER 10

The Reverend Hedley J. Williams had been rector of St. George's Episcopal Church in Arlington, Virginia for over twenty years. He was now in his early sixties, his white hair quite becoming. Standing five feet eight inches tall and with a slender build, he was a gentle and pleasant man with a smile and a sparkle that warmed every heart.

David sat in the rector's office for the usual initial conversation between a field work supervisor and a new seminarian about to come on board. Discussion centered on the history, ministry, and style of the parish and how a new team member might best fit in. At least it was normal until Hedley asked David what he thought he might like to do in the fall to start out his two-year program.

"I have no idea whatsoever," David answered. "I have never had a responsible adult position in the church. All my activity to date has been with acolytes, junior choir, Sunday school, and youth groups. That's been fine and fun, but again, I've had no experience with any adult role like lay reader or vestry. So I really don't know where to begin."

"Okay," said the rector. "Then let's use that to the best advantage we can. We'll tie down the Sunday morning responsibilities of service participation first, and take up other specifics later. You may want to sit in on an adult class, Sunday school class, or youth group, just to see where you might best fit in, and then pick and choose from there. Sound all right?"

"That sounds fine to me," the future staff member said, "but are you sure that you're not just bending over backwards for me? I wouldn't want you to sacrifice what another seminarian could do better just to help out a beginner like me."

"Don't worry about that," the older man beamed. "I'll get work out of you."

They both chuckled, then parted company for the time being. The two of them had convened on the same day Bob had his meeting with Father Andrews at St. Andrew's. John, of course, did not need any kind of initial meeting since he already had a working relationship with the Reverend Ed Sims at St. Francis in Potomac, Maryland, and had, in fact, already begun working with the youth group there.

The aforementioned meetings took place on Monday, February 10th. Two days later the season of Lent was to begin. That Ash Wednesday found them all in chapel for the first service of the day, which was not the norm. Bob was a regular attendee, but John and David were not morning people. David usually got up for breakfast and then lay back down for an hour or so before getting ready for class. John just slept in.

But that day was a special time, as well as being a holy day of obligation. So they began it together on the nave's front row, gospel side, confessing their sins and asking for strength to lead more godly lives. Giving up something for Lent as a symbol of sacrifice was a long standing tradition in the life of the Christian church. But more recently the idea of taking on some special task or commitment had become popular. David chose to work in the refectory on Sunday evenings, helping to prepare the weekly buffet dinner. John agreed to take on the responsibility of serving as the dorm nurse, and Bob volunteered to work in the library.

As solemn and disciplined a season as Lent was supposed to be, it did not preclude the celebration of certain feasts. St. Valentine's Day that year came just two days after Ash Wednesday, so that Friday night presented the community with its annual party. Because of their notoriety from "Genesis: Once Over Lightly," David and John had been asked to write the skit for the evening. They gave it their best shot, and the result was entitled "The St. Valentine's Day Massacre."

The action unfolded with Ginny Seminary, portrayed by Bob, dancing across the stage. Behind her then came two men named Big Spike and Little Pike, portrayed by John and David, doing a Keystone Cops routine. Running in sync with one another, they grabbed Ginny and exited. With the theme from *Mission: Impossible* playing, the second scene opened, and a character performed by Ed clicked on a tape player.

"Good morning, Mr. Helps," said the voice on tape. "What you just saw were two members of Hell's Anglicans kidnapping humble, lowly, liturgical Ginny Seminary. Your mission, which you had better accept or we'll kill you, is to rescue her. If you or any member of your God Squad fails, those who are in positions of authority will disavow any knowledge of your transgressions. This tape will self-destruct in five seconds."

Well, it went on from there. Different students made spoofs of different faculty members, and everyone took it in the spirit of fun. Certainly it was no great work of art, but it did come off well. Applauded for their effort, John and Duck retired to their rooms after helping to clean up Scott Lounge, where the action had taken place. They both slept well that night.

Lent and winter progressed, and before long it was again time to study for finals. With the exception of a couple of good movies, like *The Shoes of the Fisherman* and *The Lion in Winter*, there were no major distractions from the everyday academic pursuit of knowledge.

Exam week went well, and the overall average of our central characters was a solid "B." Although the grades were good, enthusiasm was less so because many members of the class were beginning to wonder if there was anything more to theological education than just books. Clinical training and field education seemed to offer a change of pace in the future, but for the present, the break at the end of the term amounted to a welcome respite from a somewhat monotonous routine. As David departed for Roanoke, his hope and his prayer was that in so many ways, the third quarter would be a season of rebirth for everyone.

Spring did indeed bring new life. As flowers blossomed and trees budded in the spirit of resurrection, March came in with a sense of renewal for the academic year. Once again, required subjects were offered in the Old Testament, focusing on the people of God in Israel; New Testament classes centered on the Gospel of John. Electives came from language and biblical study of the later epistles. Class lectures were still given in the mornings with only slight variation, and for the most part the instructors remained the same.

Once things got under way, the days overflowed with seeing and visiting with people again, in addition to getting back into the habit of study. Roy Green and Henry

Witten were often visitors to Wilmer Hall for late night conversations, and familiar means of recreation were alive and well—like playing cards, playing piano, and seeing movies.

Two political figures captured the world's news that month. On March 17th, Golda Meir became the prime minister of Israel, and on March 28th former President Dwight David Eisenhower died at the age of seventy-eight. But nothing seemed to take precedent for either David or his dorm buddies over one reality: Patty was coming to visit during Holy Week.

The sun shone brightly in a cloudless sky as Patricia Ann Magill and her mother departed Chattanooga for Atlanta on Saturday, March 29th—the day before Holy Week was to begin—to connect to I-85/I-95, which they followed up to Washington. They had planned to stay with a good friend of Patty's mother in Arlington, Virginia, and the upcoming visit plus many other things were on their minds as the two women chatted in their mother-daughter way.

Patty was a sophomore in college and full of life. Her sorority had just won the annual follies skit, and she also had a lot to share with David about her experiences with the bishop, for she herself was working with Vander Horst on a project to build a new house for the campus Canterbury Club, of which she was the president.

There was no question that Patty was a most attractive lady, made more so by her long, brown hair. She had been letting it grow ever since she began dating David steadily at the University of Chattanooga in the fall of 1967. That they were quite attracted to each other and compatible in many ways was evident, so much so that the two of them were thinking both independently and corporately about what their life might be like together. Nevertheless, when

David left for Virginia, the two of them had decided that it was not time to make a commitment to each other since each had career trainings to pursue in separate locations.

Exiting onto Glebe Road, the same one that David took each Sunday morning to St. George's, they soon arrived at the home of Mil Ritchie. After sipping a cold Coke, Patty called David to let him know she was in. She had not yet seen *Oliver!* And Duck couldn't wait to treat her to the movie, so he hurried right over. Needless to say, they were more than glad to see each other again.

Palm Sunday came early for David since he wanted to get an idea of what the eight o'clock service was like at St. George's. But soon thereafter he was at Mil's house, bidding both her and Patty's mom a cordial hello along with a prayer for a most meaningful Holy Week. Patty looked as lovely as ever, and David later beamed as he introduced her to members of his parish.

Sunday afternoon was usually a rest time for seminarians, but David had no intention of missing a moment with his girl. He and Patty brunched at the International House of Pancakes up the street, drove around Washington for a while, and wound up that night back in time to meet Ed in his room for *Mission: Impossible*. Bob, John, and Roy were also present, and they all later assured David that they more than approved of his choice in women.

During the following week while David was in class, Patty toured Washington with her mother and Mil. But the nights belonged to David. Monday, Tuesday, and Wednesday evenings, they enjoyed dinner together, then took in a movie. Each night they also took time to share their affection. While they were still not ready to make a permanent commitment to each other, they both admitted that their feelings were growing stronger.

After Wednesday evening's movie, they stood outside of Wilmer Hall and threw stones at the construction site of the new continuing education building, which was being built adjacent to the dorm just off of the refectory. All of a sudden, he began to laugh.

"What is it?" Patty asked.

David told her that looking at the construction site had just reminded him what took place a couple of weeks before. The beginning of spring had allowed the Wilmer-ites to open their entry doors to welcome in the warmer weather in the evening hours. One night Bruce Myers, who lived on the first floor across from Bob, heard something scratching at the bottom of his door. From where he had positioned his bed, he was able to reach the knob and open his door without getting up. There he found himself staring into the face of a very large rat, one that had ventured over from its uprooted home in the new building area. Needless to say, Bruce slammed the door, and after that, the entry-level screen doors always remained shut.

"And that's the saga of the one we not-so-affectionately refer to as Ralph Rat," David said.

"Ugh," said Patty. "I do not care for rats!"

And with a chuckle followed by a loving embrace, the two of them parted company until the next day.

In the second half of Holy Week, the mood of the gospel accounts shifts to a much more somber tone. That was also true for the 1969 VTS juniors. On the morning of Maundy Thursday, most of the members were present in chapel for the reading of a traditional epistle to the seminary community. That occasion was always used to hear an honest assessment of how the class perceived itself at that point in time.

At the appropriate point in the service, class president Ken Henry approached the lectern to read the following communication:

> Where am I? Drifting or stabilized? God knows! You don't! A stormy sea of tangled thoughts—reaching, groping. Lost? No! But searching. The holy hill is a battleground, a source of extreme tension and ecstatic joy, a nucleus of need. Faculty, where are you? Learned and real, high and mighty, sharing and caring? Just let me know! Grind me, push me, pull me, but don't quit on me! Who are you? Who cares! Perhaps I do. But the clichés don't work, the relevant phonies are out to lunch. See me where I am, don't box me out. I want you—with all of your love and hate, trust and doubt, acceptance and rejection. High church, low church, middle, all or no church—see me! I'm grabbing for you and for life. Spin your wheels. Grab a cross and get a handful of splinters. But together let us step into now! 'This is the generation of them that seek Him.'

After a pregnant pause, Ken continued:

> I thank God for this epistle, for in its formation, this junior class sincerely tried to find itself. In this unique process, our many differences became oh-so-evident—married and single, community and isolation, meeting and turning away. We found how human we really are, how full of failure, and yet how very much alike. We never gave each other the sweet Jesus bit. We gave ourselves. With biting remarks and slushy tolerance, a new awareness

emerged. There was love. Threatened? Certainly!
Challenged? Maybe! Dead? Never! Hope? Forever!
We find that discovering the Gospel, and therein
ourselves, is a shattering and thrilling experience.
Amen.

Ken sat down. Another moment of silence ensued while
the members of the congregation tried to digest what they
had just heard. There was no question, even as cryptic as
the reading was in many ways, that a most moving experience had just taken place. In the assembly of the Christian
community, in the company of faculty and students alike,
a select group of people had been honest about where they
were in the development of their faith, and it became clear
that the present body of Christ at VTS had arrived with
disparate motivations. For the rest of the day, the entire
community seriously reflected and wrestled with the inher-
ent question of where they were in the progression of their
own personal religion.

Bob, David, and John were obviously no strangers to
that query. Along with so many others that day, they too
wondered how they best could assess the ways in which they
were traveling down the road of their own relationships
with God and how best they might manifest those truths
for the moment.

In various ways for everyone involved, that corporate
feeling carried itself into the weekly service that evening—
into the very service that commemorated the institution of
the Last Supper of our Lord and Savior Jesus Christ.

The Wilmerites themselves responded differently to the
solemnity of the occasion. For Bob, the best response in faith
that he felt he could make was by again offering his voice to
God, so once more he sang in the choir during worship. John

offered the gift of his mind by taking time before the weekly gathering to read the several gospel accounts of the final meal Jesus took with His disciples. And in the privacy of his own room before joining his comrades, David offered the gift of himself by having his own personal communion with the Lord, sitting at his desk and consuming a Ritz cracker and a small glass of water. Not meant to be a substitute for the sacrament he was later to receive, it was simply intended to be a prayerful and intimate expression of re-commitment. That's what all three of them were doing really, and what others had done throughout the day as well—rededicating themselves to God.

David sat with Patty, John, Ed, and Roy for the celebration of Holy Communion. For all of them, the service became not only a culmination of the events of the day, but also a most solemn introduction to the events of Good Friday that were to follow.

The next day there were no classes, allowing each member of the corporate body time to assimilate the profound offering that had been made by the Son of God on behalf of the entire human race, an offering designed to take away the sins of the world. Responses varied from early morning prayers to sleeping late.

Patty and David had a late breakfast together, spent some time with Mil and Mrs. Magill, and that night went to see the 1959 classic film *Ben-Hur* at the new L'Enfant Plaza Theater. Perhaps it was not the most orthodox of ways to commemorate Good Friday, but it was a meaningful expression for the two of them.

It also for all practical purposes was the last expression of her visit, for Patty departed the next morning. Upon her return to Chattanooga, she called to say that she had arrived home safely. David went to bed thankful that she was okay and that it was less than two months before he would see her again.

"When are you going to marry that girl?" Bob asked, posing the question that was on the minds of every dorm dweller.

There was no question about their favorable impression of Patty, as well as their observation of her effect on David, one which he did not yet realize was that strong.

"Not sure," David replied. "Bishop Vander Horst asked me not to consider matrimony until after seminary."

"That's a long time," John chimed in.

"Yea, I know."

The next day our central characters celebrated Easter together at the Washington National Cathedral.

CHAPTER 11

Oliver! did quite well at the Academy Awards on the night of April 8th, and three particular residents of Wilmer Hall were very pleased. They and several other members of the dorm had gathered around Ed's color television for the event with pizza, beer, and a general mood of gaiety. It was a pleasant experience that carried them through the weekend—alone, for most of the class was attending a retreat at Peterkin Conference Center in Romney, West Virginia. Bob, David, and John had been turned off by the questionnaire sent to them by the conference leaders, which focused on the theme of seeking "The Impossible Dream."

It appeared that the sessions would be designed for those who wanted a change from the hill and academic life, who wanted a non-seminary atmosphere, who wanted to leave behind the monotony of routine, who wanted to share experiences and ideas in small groups, and who wanted some recreational activities as well.

None of those agenda items appealed much to the trio of friends who had stayed behind. It seemed somewhat ironic to them that the very things the rest of the class was looking for were things that they already had. Why go away to talk about broadening and deepening relationships, when it seemed a better use of time to stay right where they were and continue to live more and more into what they had already started.

After all, those three members of the junior class had already begun to explore their feelings with one another, risk being alive with one another, listen to and share in the lives of one another, and delve into the problems and issues that they thought they might face in their future ministries. Going away some place for a weekend was not necessary when they were already living in community with one another.

Classes resumed the following week at the same time that the $150 clinical training fee was due for the summer session. David and John were glad to know that the withdrawal from their checking accounts had not affected their plans to live out what was to be the first of three spring trips to Manhattan. The Metroliner (an express train between Washington and New York) had just begun service, and the two thought that traveling its full route by rail from DC to the "Big Apple" would be fun.

The Thursday night before their departure was like all nights before vacations—full of anticipation and gusto. They had put a lot of time into the planning before John made the final arrangements. The two friends had researched what Broadway shows they wanted to see, where they wanted to eat, and just how they wanted to spend their time.

So after chapel, David and John along with Bob and Roy departed for their favorite pizza spot since the failure of Chuck's Carry-Out. It was a place called The Village Inn, an old hamlet style building with banjos and silent movies playing and the best pizza, beer, and blue cheese salad dressing that any of them had ever tasted. Bob and Roy were likewise in a celebratory mood, even though they were not going on the trip, and as an old favorite was offered by one of the banjo players, the group joined together in four-part harmony. It didn't sound bad at all.

After the evening ritual of tapping on radiators to say good night, the two future travelers slept well and awoke to the first day of their weekend adventure. Since the Metroliner did not depart until 3:00 on the afternoon of April 18th, they decided to take the 1:45 local. But when the local did not arrive until thirty minutes after the new train was scheduled to get in, they learned the value of taking the "express."

Nevertheless, they had arrived in New York. John and David took a cab to the Taft Hotel, where David had stayed in 1961 on his first and only other trip to Manhattan. The two checked in, but found they could only get two single rooms on different halls of a high floor where they could wave to each other across a long drop to the "beautiful" alley below. But since they were going to spend the majority of their time away from the rooms anyway, it really did not matter very much.

After freshening up, then having a quick bite at the hotel grill, the friends walked to the Helen Hayes Theater for the 8:00 p.m. performance of the drama *Hadrian VII*. Following their first Broadway play together, the two walked over to Times Square to take in the lights, and after returning to the Taft, enjoyed a full dinner back at the hotel grill.

Saturday, the out-of-towners went to visit a friend of John's at General Theological Seminary over on the west side of town. That was followed by the matinée performance at Radio City Music Hall, which consisted of three parts—the spring production; the Easter pageant; and the Disney film, *The Love Bug*. They had not anticipated the long line, however, so David came up with a stunt he hoped would work.

He strode to the front door and asked the head usher, "Are we supposed to enter from the side?"

David was as surprised as anyone to hear his answer. "Yes."

So, the tourists went around to the side door, told the junior usher that the head usher had told them to go in there, and they were allowed access ahead of over two hundred people. Cagey? Yes, but effective. Therefore, they success-fully managed to enjoy a fabulous presentation in one of the largest and nicest theaters in the world.

That night the two of them dined at The Brass Rail and went to see the musical *George M!* at the Palace Theater. After a snack, our big city visitors decided there was enough time to take a late ferry cruise over to Staten Island and back. But because the evening hours offered sailing only once every hour rather than every half hour, they were quite late in returning to their hotel rooms.

One thing they discovered in riding on the subway after midnight, unfortunately, was the reality of the homeless sit-uation in New York and how often policemen had to remove people from the cars who were looking for a place to sleep.

Arising at ten o'clock on Sunday morning, David and John ate breakfast, then checked out of the hotel. They had left themselves enough time to spend the early afternoon atop the Empire State Building, affording them their final opportunity of the trip to view the city they had just visited. Then, from Penn Station, our adventurers departed on the 4:15 Metroliner for Washington. Their original choice of travel was a comfortable and pleasant ride that took just under three hours. Bob was there to meet them at Union Station and to drive them home in Flo.

For the remaining five weeks of the first academic year, life seemed to speed up faster with each passing week. It was hard to believe that the months had gone by so quickly, and that the milestone of having completed one-third of seminary loomed on the horizon. Bob, David, and John now found themselves noticing the members of the senior class more and more—those who were preparing to leave VTS and "go into all the world and preach the gospel." That prospect seemed frightening to the juniors. Were those folks really ready? And two years from now, would they be ready? Thank God, graduation still seemed to be a long way off.

The last thirty-five days were not without their profound moments. The first was the death of an aged faculty member. Walter Russell Bowie died in late April, just after an autograph party for his new book, "Learning to Live."

The second eventful moment took place on the last day of the month. There was a new presence on the hill, one that would be there for years to come—the newly elected dean. Granville Cecil Woods Jr. from Tennessee was the choice of the community as a whole. He came to campus to look the place over, as well as talk with professors and students alike. David actually knew the new dean personally. He had been David's baby-sitter in bygone days, as well as being a friend of his college dean at the University of Chattanooga.

The student protests happening on almost every campus across America were shaking up the traditional hierarchy of academe. It was a little different at VTS. Having gained creative participation in the decision-making process for the election of the new dean, the student body then wanted membership on faculty committees and the right to suggest changes in the curriculum.

"It's just not right," Bob argued. "Students shouldn't be making decisions or even suggestions about anything until they have been through the entire process."

"That's just not where everyone else seems to be," John and David replied.

David soon found himself serving on the Student Aid Society, an organization funded by voluntary contributions and designed to aid confidentially those in the community in need of financial assistance. The Tennessean was grateful for the sense of responsibility it gave him.

On a lighter note, Henry Witten and Bob's constant jokes about the girth of the other had led to a friendly competition. Bob was pleased to become the junior class leader in weight loss—down some twenty-six pounds.

The balmy days of May arrived and brought several items of note. Several of the dorm dwellers started their suntans, lying out on the rooftops of their respective buildings. The long awaited cassock and surplice combinations ordered back in January finally arrived, and the Wilmerites carefully packed them away for retrieval in the fall when field work would commence. Each had met again with their future supervisors and signed off on initial letters of agreement for their twelve hour per week contracts starting in September.

There were a couple of social events early in the month— another dance, then the second student council picnic of the year. David's social life focused mainly on talking with and writing to Patty, congratulating her on being accepted into X-ray technology school, and giving thanks that time was ticking closer to when they would get to see each other again.

The month of May also brought faculty recommendations and applications for candidacy, the next step after postulancy in the ordination process for seminarians. A dorm picnic closed out the year socially just before finals began on Monday, the 19th. The trio of friends came through all their exams just fine.

Since campus was crowded for the week of commencement with a number of visitors, the members of the junior class were asked to vacate the premises early, even before graduation. Saturday, May 24th, the day after finals ended, was coincidentally John's twenty-fourth birthday. So another surprise party was in the offing as the year's farewell gathering for Bob, David, and John. Partially as a ruse, David invited John to join him for *Support Your Local Sheriff* at the Center Theater just down the road from campus. Meanwhile Bob, Ed, Jim, and Roy readied for the party back at the dorm, acquiring cards, cake, and pizza. The party concluded by watching a Mae West and W.C. Fields movie on the late show.

After things broke up, John asked David if he could copy his Peter, Paul, and Mary tape to play on his drive home. It was one of three David had made so far on the machine he had bought earlier from Bruce Myers.

"Are you sure you don't want copies of Petula Clark and Glen Campbell too?" David questioned.

"No, I'll be fine with PP&M. Hey listen," said John, extending his hand to his friend. "You take care of yourself—and Patty as well."

"Yeah, you too. I'll especially look forward to taking care of Patty."

They both laughed, knowing their friendship would miss time together over the next three months, but each would eagerly await resumption in the fall. As they bid each other Godspeed, they wondered in the back of their minds just how much their clinical training over the summer would change them.

The next day, the single students locked up their rooms for the summer. For Bob, David, and Ed the closing was a more arduous task since they were all able to move upstairs

onto John's floor due to vacancies there caused by graduation. The prospect of living on the same floor was a move
all were eager to make and knowing that their community
would naturally grow stronger because of it made it easier
to say good-bye.

Everyone loaded up then and drove off in his respective
direction. As David traveled down I-81, he began to compose
in his mind the Ember Day letter he would soon mail to his
bishop.

> Well, my first year is over. The time has passed
> all too fast. I have learned much and have much to
> learn. A year ago at this time I was quite curious as
> to what type of life I would encounter at seminary.
> And now I have discovered that life is just as real in
> Virginia as it is anywhere. You don't have to go into
> the ghetto to see people in trouble, sorrow, or need.
> I've seen it right there at VTS. And I have seen hap-
> piness—the type of happiness that can come from
> friendships formed and lasting relationships made.
> The answer to the question of life seems to lie in
> people. In my first year, I think that I have had a
> small taste of what life is all about.

CHAPTER 12

Although they did not have much time together before his summer session began, David and Patty made the most of what they had, including a trip to Atlanta to see some shows. But before too long, communication between them once again took place by telephone and letter. On June 19th, David wrote to his sweetheart:

> So, I'm alive and well in Memphis, and after a week and a half of clinical training, I am fully convinced it is a worthwhile program. I am learning much about myself, about other people, and about the relationship between the two.
>
> I'm sitting here watching television. My room is fairly nice. I share it with another seminarian in the program by the name of Bob Pelrine. We have two beds, two closets, and a chest of drawers, but we are also using the connecting room—the surgeon resident's office—which is seldom needed. It has a lavatory, TV, desk, and phone; so, all in all, we are doing pretty well.
>
> There are six people in the program—three Episcopalians, two Catholics, and one Presbyterian. Bob, my roommate, is one of the Catholics.
>
> Since I got in about 4:30 on Sunday, June 8th, it

has been a pleasure getting to know both the routine and the people, especially Bill Patten from my home parish, whom I had never known very well before.

The first full day, Monday the 9th, we spent in orientation. Since then, we have taken a tour of our hospital, visited an alcoholics' ward at the VA Hospital, which we will do every week, and become familiar with program procedure.

The main focus of the course is visitation and consultation. We go from 8:30–4:30 Monday through Friday, and pretty much plan our own day. We choose the patients we wish to see, write verbatim reports on our visits, and discuss them in seminars. Add to that an individual conference each week with the supervisor of the program, as well as chances to observe hospital routine, and it makes for quite a learning opportunity. The food is not bad. I've seen several films, and so far am enjoying life here.

David closed his epistle with some personal notes, signed it with love, and then sealed the letter in its envelope. Writing his return address on the back, he paused to notice the title that preceded his name, "Chaplain."

Looking hard at it for a few moments, David acknowledged that it was not just a title he had decided to put on the letter. For the next few weeks, he would indeed be a chaplain. Realizing that fact after the first session of the seminar, it dawned on him that the summer session would have a lot to offer as far as opportunity was concerned. It would also be a time to finally deal with a lot of personal questions.

It would be a time to take a good look at himself—where he had been, where he was in his life, and where he was going from there. It would be a time to take what he was learning in a theological graduate school and use it to try and help people in the real world. The summer would be a time to begin being a minister, rather than just exploring the possibilities of it.

To say that the weeks ahead would be difficult was an understatement for the members of the clinical training group assembled in Memphis. They soon discovered that there were no tailor-made answers given to the questions they posed, no easy answers offered as to just exactly how God relates with His people and vice versa.

There was always a great deal of emotions with which to grapple, not only with the patients but also among and within the chaplains themselves. But as the team players came to know one another better, as they came to understand their strengths and weaknesses, and as they came to accept themselves as they were, each one came to realize more and more the profound truth of what had been drilled into them over and over—that there indeed were no simple answers to the serious questions in life. The real task seemed to be in making sure one asked the right questions so that prayerfully one might then know which direction to guide their charges toward. David missed his seminary colleagues and wondered how they were dealing with those same issues in their respective locales.

Fortunately, the summer also held moments of ease and comfort with friends and loved ones. Bill Patten and David attended Sunday services at the cathedral. Charlie Jones was a friend and fraternity brother of David's who was in medical school in Memphis, and the two of them enjoyed a good deal of time together, especially the July Fourth weekend—one of several times when Patty and Charlie's girlfriend Janice Datres drove over for dates, dinners, and movies. Also there were conversations with the doctors, like

Allen Hughes, with whom David watched the moon landing on July 20th and from whom he learned the rudiments of banjo picking.

Also the following things took place while the world revolved that June, July, and August: *Hee-Haw* premiered on CBS. Warren Burger took the oath of office as the Supreme Court's fifteenth Chief Justice. The Category 5 hurricane known as Camille slashed the Gulf Coast, killing 259 people and galvanizing Americans to give with open hearts to the victims of the second strongest hurricane in U.S. history. John Wayne played Rooster Cogburn in the much-loved western *True Grit*, and the three-day Woodstock "peace and music" festival hosted upwards of 400,000 young people in New York's rainy Catskill Mountains, forever changing music history. All that, plus David was approved for candidacy.

During the summer of 1969 medicine and religion waged war on the same battleground of life at the West Tennessee Chest Disease Hospital in Memphis. In his final report, David tried to summarize creatively the depths of his summer experience.

Reflections On The Sixteenth Chapter Of Job, Wherein He Complains Of God's Hostility

I am weary—very weary. Another day has come, and still I am here; still my body lies immobile. It seems that as long as I can remember I have waked to stare at four walls—three walls and a window perhaps, but even that window is a wall, for the picture is always the same. So is my life, confined to this bed, made of monotony, loneliness, hell. I cannot even remember the wreck. I remember not the time nor the place nor the event. I only know that it changed my life. It killed my legs. It killed me. I will never walk again. I think back over my life. I think of the joy and happiness. I think of the pleasures, never to realize that such small and simple things might never come again.

People come; they are sorry that it happened. People go; they forget me. My God, if they only knew what it was really like—day after day after day. They are "sorry." What does that mean to me? They stay a minute; I stay for life. Why did this happen to me? What did I do to deserve all this? What kind of a God would let this happen? I begin to see for the first time how real those questions can be, now that I am the one who lies in the hospital bed. I think back to those days at clinical training ten years ago. I think back to those people that I encountered. I think of the times that I sat with people as they cried. What did their lives mean to me? Oh, what a miserable comforter I was! I had no idea what it was like.

I tried to listen. I tried to be of use—to sympathize and feel and help. But how hard that really was to do! What could I have really meant to them? But then I think of what the lives of those who come to me mean. Is it not enough that they just come? That, I can appreciate. But no one can really help me. This is it; this is my life. Why? I do not know, and those who visit me fumble for answers.

The same question prevails—why? I do not know.

Where do I turn? Others cannot comfort me. I cannot even comfort myself. What else is there? Perhaps . . . God? Is it not He who has done this to me? No. The answer is not so simple that I may merely blame someone else—and alas it is not God. It is life—this life of chance and love and hate and war and peace and fear and hope and on and on and on. That is what has done this. That, in itself, is life. My God! The risks we take every day! Can one really imagine what they are till he becomes susceptible to them?

Perhaps that is the hell of it. I am susceptible to life. I have heard people cry out in this life, "How can there be a God?" As I think more and more, I ask, "How can there not be?" I myself will never walk again. I cannot answer why. But, oh, if that were the end of it, if my only hopes lie in poor attempts by friends to comfort me, if my only hopes lie in my poor attempts to comfort myself, if my only hopes lie in mere acceptance of the fact that I was and am and will be this way, it would be hell.

Is that escape? Is that not accepting reality? Is that copping out? I think not. It cannot be. The escape and the refusal and the copping out would come if my trust only went as far as myself. I must go that far, for that is life, and I cannot put that aside. But if that were all there was, it would be hell. Why? The reason for pain, for suffering— what is it? I do not know; I cannot answer; man cannot answer. Only something—no someone—greater than man could answer. God help me, I realize that I cannot even answer the questions of my own life.

I think back to clinical training; I think back to the encounter group where we tore off layers of our

*defenses. How hard it was and how long it took to
only begin to see a sliver of oneself. And now, how
long is life? I can never answer all the questions of
life. I can never answer all the questions of others.
I can never answer all the questions of myself. But
can I not begin?*

The dream ended there. I awoke, indeed, in a
hospital but not as a patient. I was a chaplain. I had
ten days left in my first quarter of clinical pastoral
education. Although clinical training was nearly over,
I was only beginning to learn.

In the dream I was Job. I wondered why. Something I had never had to do before. I had been with
Jobs before. I had been with those who wondered
why. But in the dream it was *me*. The nightmare of
being the patient had made me see something. What
had been my purpose in coming to this place? It was
a requirement of the seminary. It was an opportunity to find out some things about myself. It was an
opportunity to work with other people, other lives.
What is my purpose now? It has become a ministry.

I have seen many people. I have seen them when
they were sick, disabled, and tired. I have seen people
in need—people crying for help. And I am not in their
place. I cannot really identify with the hell that they
are going through. Can I help? I only witness. They
have to live with it. What comfort can I offer them?
I do not know. I pray to God. Each of those people
has a life as real to them as mine is to me. I dream
of the horror of physical illness and disfigurement.
I live with those for whom it is reality. Can I help?
Perhaps I'll never really know the answer to that
question, just as I will never know the answer to the

reason for pain. Can I help?

People search for answers. They look. The patients, the chaplains, the encounter group—we all look for answers. We all look for self-understanding. And by that, we find how to understand others. And it helps. I know that it has helped me. I know what others can mean and have meant to me. I need others. I need to offer myself to others. The next step then, hopefully, would be their needing me.

Need seems to be the one thing that we all have in common. Man looks for something beyond himself. He cannot answer the questions alone. So he turns to those around him. Together we search. We will never find out all of the answers. We may find part of them. But prayerfully, we will find a need and fulfillment in one another, which is love.

And love can only lead us onward to one greater than we are, in whom all those puzzle pieces fit together. Without Him none of it makes sense. The questions and the goals that we have in life will lead us to God. And if what has been detailed above can be defined as love, then the path to it can be no better exemplified than by Christ.

I begin to understand myself a little better. I begin to understand others a little better. I know we all have much in common. And I believe that when we try to communicate, we do so by the power of the Holy Spirit of God.

I think that is the reason for my ministry—to be human—to search, to love, to find. Someday we may find out the answer altogether. Perhaps that is heaven.

THE MIDDLER YEAR

CHAPTER 13

P atty and David didn't even have as much time to spend
together after the chaplaincy program as they did
before it started. On Wednesday, September 3rd, his
father's fifty-first birthday, David left home again for school
in Virginia. As he drove, he thought about how much longer
a trip it had been the year before in so many ways, but that
wasn't the case anymore. Roanoke seemed to come quickly,
as did the Travel Lodge and a movie. Although he slept
late—almost till noon—he managed to arrive back on the
VTS campus by 5:00 on Thursday.

He had enough time to settle into his new room on the
second floor of Wilmer Hall, #207, before attending the welcome back picnic, usually held outside of the refectory. Rain
forced everyone inside, so it was not the most attractive day
to begin, especially for members of the new junior class, who
were experiencing the same growing pains that the central
characters of our story had experienced the year before.

As David walked over to the dining room, he noticed a
big change that had taken place over the summer months.
The circle next to his dorm, where the residents had parked
the year before, had vanished because of the completion of
the new continuing education building.

That fact was quickly lost on him, however, for as soon
as he opened the refectory door, he heard a most familiar

and drawn out "Well!" David turned to spot Bob's stocky frame waddling toward him. A fond embrace brought back all the memories of their first year together in an instant, and though they had written to one another from their respective clinical sites, it was apparent that they had missed each other more than words on paper could express.

"How was the summer?" David queried.

"Ugh!" was the only response Bob could make.

A chuckle of mutual understanding passed between them as the grueling sensitivity training of the encounter group sessions flashed in their minds. Then to escape the memories that were painful, they hastened into the company of others to exchange hearty greetings and offer superficial reflections on the pros and cons of the summer program. The festivities broke up at about 7:30, and those who had found old friends and those who had discovered new ones returned to their respective homes-away-from-home for the next nine months.

As those in his dorm began to unpack and arrange their rooms, Bob treated them all to a rendition of one of Verdi's operas by turning up the volume on his record player so that the music might offer a welcoming note for one and all.

"Good grief," a voice was heard to say. "I sure wish you could hear yourself think on this floor."

As John opened the door to room #204, more embraces ensued. It was indeed a special moment as Chamberlain, Redmon, and McCann renewed their acquaintance while they carried in the last of their bags. After the luggage was dropped off, work ceased for the remainder of the day, because there was just too much to talk about. Pretty soon several cars departed for Lums, the three middlers being followed by several juniors who were anxious to discover local hot spots. Not long afterward, fellow Wilmerites Bruce

Myers and Rich Pocalyko joined the party. Lumburgers with beer were the order of the evening as old relationships and new ones began to coincide. Before long, old and new alike felt they had come home.

It was a good entry into the second year for John, David, and Bob. The majority of their conversation, of course, focused on various summer experiences. The new students were interested in hearing about the program they so far knew very little about. But soon thoughts turned toward the future for all of them.

"I think this will be the best year of all," John said on the way back to the dorm. "We're no longer the new kids on the block, but we don't have to worry yet about where we're going after graduation like the seniors do."

Bob and David concurred, and with that shared feeling of contentment about the next nine months, they all prepared to turn in around 11:30. Bob said good night first, and closed his door, leaving the other two standing at the entrances to their rooms.

"Wait a minute," said David. "How are we going to say good night to each other since we're now on the same floor, and the radiator communication system won't work any longer?"

John smiled, raised his hand in the gesture of making the sign of the cross in the same manner that he hoped to bless others in the future as a priest. David returned both the smile and the gesture. Without verbal agreement, they both understood that they would be using that benediction at bedtime as long as they were together.

The following day things got into full swing. Course registration with Dr. Reid began in Packard-Laird Auditorium at 9:20, which was followed by a coffee break at 10:30. David, Bob, and John, beamed when they ran into Ed, Jim, and

Roy again, as well as other favorite friends. Sessions with the business manager finished off the morning.

Friday afternoon was spent getting the dorm rooms back in order, and at 6:00 the entire community gathered together for dinner and the opening service of the year. Chaplain Phil Smith celebrated Holy Communion, and the new dean, Cecil Woods, preached his first sermon in that role.

"When one returns home after years of being away," the new headmaster began, "he must expect and be prepared for change. . . ."

John looked down at the campus newspaper *Ambo,* which he had brought in with him. Just who was the man who had come to lead Virginia Theological Seminary into the future? He scanned a brief biography:

> The Very Reverend Granville Cecil Woods, Jr., came to VTS from Sewanee, Tennessee, where he was the rector of Otey Memorial Parish and also a member of the faculty and chaplain of St. Luke's Seminary, the School of Theology at the University of the South. . . . After several years of wartime service in the air force and of college teaching, he entered VTS and received a bachelor of divinity degree in 1953. Following three years of parish experience, he went to Yale Divinity School and received a master of sacred theology degree in 1958. The Dean also spent two years at Oxford University in England where he studied 19th century theology. . . .

John looked up from the article to return his attention to the sermon. The dean's comments about the present challenges faced by the church captivated him—as they did Bob and David.

I am convinced that the task of theological education has never been more delicate or more crucial.
The church is faced with a range of problems, inter-
nal and external, which seem too numerous and too
intractable to be endured, much less resolved.

The temptations to faithlessness were never
greater. We are invited, urged, lured by despairing
and misguided persons within the church, as well
as by sincere critics without, to give up. There are
many ways of 'copping out,' psychologically speaking;
there always have been. But the greater danger, in
my opinion, is for the church, in and for our time, out
of confusion and bewilderment, to 'cop out' theolog-
ically speaking.

As one of the intellectual centers of the church
on this continent, we have the duty not only to seek
the truth rigorously, with radical honesty, but to test
all that we know or think we know in the purifying
fire of critical analysis. Certainly, we are aware that
we, individually, and the church, collectively, have
been wrong and neglectful in many matters both
intellectual and moral. Our knowledge of God and of
man is incomplete and imperfect; in will, as well as
in intellect, we are defective. Nevertheless, to speak
and act as if the church has no vital gospel for the
world, as if we have experienced nothing of meaning
and value, as if we know nothing and bear witness
to no One is not only faithless; it is false.

The primary responsibility of Virginia Seminary
and of other seminaries of the church in our time, in
my opinion, is this: Through the Divine self-disclo-
sure—in word, in sacrament, in the koinonia, and
in past and present history—to know the God who

is and who acts, as Creator, Redeemer, and Sancti-
fier; knowing and adoring Him, to keep the essential
Faith, as far as in us lies, of the Holy Catholic Church,
seeking new forms of language, thought, worship,
and social action in which to express this apostolic
faith in and for our time; and in gratitude for our
creation and redemption to be enabled to respond
to God's love, loving and serving God by loving and
serving His people.

This responsibility cannot be fulfilled in the contemporary cultural context without insights derived
from the new sciences of man and from contemporary
art forms; nor can it be fulfilled apart from profound
and continuing involvement with the world.

Dean Woods concluded his message and stepped down
from the pulpit, but his words lingered throughout the rest
of the service and on into the evening. Four of the Wilmerites
gathered together for late beer and pizza at The Village
Inn and discussed several sermon points that had made an
impression on them.

With his background at Humble Oil Company, Ed made
a few observations about what he thought "insights derived
from the new sciences of man" might mean as far as concerned the proclamation of the Gospel of Jesus Christ in
a modern age. Because of their love of music and movies,
both Bob and David had no question how "contemporary art
forms" could play a vital part. But it was John who made
the most significant observation by recalling one particular
word the new dean had used:

"Koinonia," McCann repeated. "That's the term that
jumped out at me more than any other. Christian community. Christian fellowship. That's what we are, and that's

what we're supposed to be. And we need to make sure we're being that right here, right now, on campus—not when we graduate and get out into the world."

"Hear, hear," David added. "But you need to know something, John, if I haven't told you this already. You were "koinonia" to me the day I arrived a year ago. You were Christian community and fellowship in action, and because you were, I'm still here to talk about it."

"And you both were to me," Bob chimed in. "That night I arrived, you two were there to welcome me into the new family I had come to join."

"Well," Ed voiced, "I may not have gotten in at the very beginning, but I sure am glad to be with you guys now."

There was a moment of silence while the last bite of pizza and the last sip of beer were consumed. Then David spoke.

"This is the first Friday night of our middler year. If you all don't have other plans, I want to propose that tomorrow night we all go out for dinner, and that henceforth we do the same on the first Friday of each month to commemorate the Christian community and fellowship we acknowledge tonight and give thanks to God that we share."

"And let's finish it off with a movie," John offered, thereby complementing Duck's suggestion by acknowledging his love of film.

So after much discussion, The Three Thieves, where the memorable meal with the Bishop of Tennessee had taken place, was chosen as the initial selection for a restaurant, and *Midnight Cowboy* at the Keith Theater in Washington was the first choice for a motion picture.

The next night, as four friends ate and talked, then sat and watched, each one arrived at the same conclusion: they were glad to be reunited.

John was ticked. For the second year in a row, his name failed to appear in the class roster section of the annual seminary catalog. Acknowledged or not, once again he found himself seated with his comrades in the ground floor class-room of Aspinwall Hall for most of their courses.

Everyone was looking forward to their first quarter classes: History of Christian Thought with Dr. Stanley, First Corinthians with Molle, Marriage and the Family with Dr. Rightor, and Early Church History with Dr. Allison. Most of the lectures were to be given in the afternoon that fall, which meant there would be more time for David and John to sleep late in the mornings.

Orientation for field education took place on Tuesday morning, September 9th. In addition to the off-site experi-ence, there was to be each week a discussion and reflection session, known as a colloquy, for which the class would be divided into small groups.

Field work began on Sunday, September 14th. By that time, all had met with their supervisors for conferences and understood their assignments for the year.

David had not only talked again with Hedley Williams but had also met with Moody Burt, the assistant rector, so he was raring to go. Although on the first day, his sole act was to administer the chalice at the celebration of Holy Communion, having been licensed by the Bishop of Virginia to do so, his duties would expand with time. Down the road he would lead a chapel service for the second through fourth grades, possibly teach a class for the ninth grade and advise the youth group, preach once a term, make visitations, and participate in both the services and organizations of the parish. At least that's what his initial learning agreement stated. And that scenario was not all that different from his contemporaries. Everybody was off and running in various directions at once.

St. George's held services on Sunday mornings at both 8:00 and 10:30. Because he and his friends had stayed up late on Saturday night watching *To Kill a Mockingbird* on TV, David had decided to skip breakfast and sleep in. By the time the last coffee hour ended at the church, he was ravenous, so he stopped in at the International House of Pancakes up the street on his drive back to Wilmer Hall.

On Tuesday the colloquy sessions met for the first time to reflect on the past Sunday's experiences. Bob and David convened in the same group with Ken Henry; John and Roy found themselves in another group with the Louisianan, Don Wimberly. In each cluster there was a member of the faculty, a clergyman, and a lay person—the latter two from parishes in the surrounding area. Meetings began at 3:15 in the afternoon and were scheduled to last as long as two hours. Most of the first sessions were spent with self-introductions, discussion of general expectations, and, as already noted, impressions of the first day.

However, the colloquies were not the highlight of that particular Tuesday, September 16th. Chaplain Smith's name was on the ballot for election as Bishop Suffragan of the Diocese of Virginia. The only other faculty member of VTS within living memory to have been elected a bishop was Robert Gibson, present diocesan and president of the board of trustees of the seminary as well, but that had happened twenty years ago. On the current ballot, twelve men had been nominated, eleven of whom were graduates of VTS. The Right Reverend Sam Chilton of the class of 1924 was

retiring. Chaplain Phil Smith of the class of 1949 was about
to take his place.

"I pray that as I live out the responsibility God is laying
on me, through you all, it will be in such a way that this
part of God's creation, where my servant ministry will be
cast, will be somewhat adequately served and His name
glorified." So wrote the decade-long faculty member as he
accepted his election as bishop suffragan, chosen that day
in Charlottesville on the fifth ballot.

For that occasion, David took the opportunity to write
his first article for *Ambo*:

> I had not seen Phil Smith all day, and it was
> only after the first middler class field education collo-
> quies that I found out why. He had just been elected
> Suffragan Bishop of the Diocese of Virginia.
>
> Something happens to you when news of that
> sort reaches your ears. This was someone whom I
> knew, someone who was close, someone whose good
> fortune created in me a desire to reach out to him
> with congratulations. I was not alone in that feeling.
>
> I had just finished supper and my nightly attempt
> at piano playing, when heading back to my dorm, I
> was approached by several of my classmates.
>
> 'Come on,' they said. 'We're going to Phil's.'
>
> That was all that was said and all that needed to
> be said. The big red chair that resided in the common
> room of Wilmer Hall was uprooted to find its next
> earthbound location to be the paved driveway of our
> dear chaplain. All the dorms were emptied and the
> faculty was summoned, everyone to congregate at
> that same place.
>
> I brought a broom. Bob Redmon painted some

signs. Jim Alby made a paper hat. The juniors decorated the house. The driveway was blocked off.

By 8:30, people were all over the yard, variously engaged as they awaited the arrival home of the guest of honor. Dr. Ross talked with the students. Dr. Graham got his camera ready. Dr. Allison put one of his big stereo speakers in the window of the Smith house, so that at the appointed time "Pomp and Circumstance" could blast into the night air.

None of us knew exactly what time Phil was scheduled to get back from the convention in Charlottesville, and it was not until 9:30 that two headlights appeared in the distance, and a car turned into the driveway. Some seventy-five people greeted Mr. and Mrs. Smith as they returned home.

Phil was escorted to his seat of honor, the big red chair, which for the moment served as a bishop's throne. My broom became his crozier. Jim's paper hat became his miter. Thus the bishop-elect was symbolically consecrated.

Cliff Stanley hugged him. Henry Rightor kidded him. Gordon Charlton shook hands with his old friend. All in all, I guess our chaplain shook hands for a good ten minutes before the crowd began to disperse.

To me, and I know to many others as well, that ten minutes was worth the two hour preparation and wait. I could have done nothing else that night that would have meant more. It was one of those rare times where everything stops and everyone comes together for a common purpose. There may be differences between faculty and students, and we may have opinions that vary about many things, but that evening our seminary community was united.

I am grateful the year started out with just such an experience. It's so refreshing to observe in action the fellowship, the friendship, and the love that Christianity is all about.

CHAPTER 14

The second half of September found everyone buckling down into the routine of study again. The members of the middler class continued to be more and more impressed with Dr. Mollegen, finding his simple homespun illustrations of gospel truth to be more profound than anything they were reading in books.

The field education colloquies were nothing to write home about, but the field work itself was proving to be most interesting and educational. David found that to be true right off the bat as he conducted the chapel service for the second through fourth grades.

On September 21st, the very first day he got the children together for worship, a small boy was chosen to light the candles. Being too short to reach the wick, the child broke into tears, feeling that he had failed to do his job.

Everyone, including the new staff seminarian, tried to comfort the small fellow, but no words were able to console him. Finally David knelt down, looked the child squarely in the eye, and simply smiled at him. Sensing that everything was all right, the lad stopped crying and smiled in return. David had begun to understand more than ever not only how actions can speak louder than words but also what the ministry of presence was all about—just being with someone could offer a blessing.

Other special events at St. George's soon followed. The adults of the congregation were justifiably concerned that no parishioner had stepped forward to teach the ninth through twelfth grades. Though David had initially thought about doing a class for the ninth grade only, he took a leap of faith by offering to convene a seminar in order for all the senior high young people to talk about whatever they wanted to discuss.

On September 28th, as he was driving in for the Sunday services, David was worried that the first seminar would bomb. He decided that he would toss out for discussion such issues as sex, drugs, and Vietnam—figuring those topics would really get things going.

But when the participants were asked what they would like to discuss, the immediate response was: "Anything but sex, drugs, and Vietnam. We're up to here with sex, drugs, and Vietnam."

David felt muzzled from the outset. But that turned out to have been the best thing that could have happened, because the future adults were free to address the concerns on which they wanted to focus, and David was freed to be a mentor and supporter of the youth, rather than another authority figure trying to get them all to go in a set direction.

The seminar was only half of the Tennessean's success in establishing an ongoing relationship with the young people of St. George's that day. After services, Mr. Chamberlain, as he was being addressed at church, stopped at IHOP once again for a late breakfast. While there, two teenagers from the parish stopped in for brunch. The three spotted each other and rearranged chairs to dine together.

Discussion picked up on the earlier morning topics, but in a much more relaxed atmosphere. That combination of seminar followed by brunch for a growing number of teens was to continue for the next two years, with David serving as the advisor for the St. George's youth group.

Back on the campus home front, other Wilmerites enjoyed sharing their own field work anecdotes. But a few other things were happening as well.

Ed had been asked to head up the special waiter squad, a group called upon from time to time to wait on the "big brass" when they came to campus, and he had invited David to serve with him. Carl Cunningham, learning of David's affection for the banjo (which had begun over the summer), lent him an old one of his so he could practice. And Bambi and Ken Henry became parents of a six pound, thirteen ounce baby girl.

Patty and David, of course, were continuing to communicate by letter and telephone. David enjoyed hearing about her studies and experiences as a student of X-ray technology, and he enjoyed sharing his campus and field work experiences, including his discussion with Hedley about possibly teaching an adult course at St. George's on the Epistle to the Galatians.

The seminarians dispatched their quarterly Ember Day letters to their respective bishops. David spent the majority of his correspondence reflecting on his summer of clinical training and his entry into the second year of seminary with a belief that ministry was becoming more clearly defined and focused in his mind, especially as he engaged in work at St. George's.

But there was something else that David needed to talk about with the Bishop of Tennessee. His letter included the following:

Although the parish ministry appeals to me much more than it has before, I still have an obligation to the armed forces as a result of my commission from the ROTC program in college; I plan to serve that time as a military chaplain, which will require at least three years of my life.

There is a nine-week chaplaincy school at Fort Hamilton in New York City next summer, which I would like to attend. I plan to write Bishop Arnold Lewis at the Office of the Bishop for the Armed Forces in the near future to begin preparation in this area.

The Right Reverend John Vander Horst acknowledged those plans in a letter David received around the first of October. Weather was beginning to turn cooler by then, and fall sniffles passed around. Bob, David, Ed, and John managed to stay well and enjoyed their second monthly outing, dining at the II Caesars in downtown DC before seeing the film *De Sade*.

That was on Friday, October 3rd, but the next Friday was a special occasion as well, and not just because it happened to be David's 23rd birthday. It was the day of the installation of the twelfth dean of Virginia Theological Seminary.

The acting president of the board of trustees, the Right Reverend David S. Rose of the Diocese of Southern Virginia, installed Cecil in the absence of Bishop Robert Gibson. And the Right Reverend John E. Hines, Presiding Bishop of the Episcopal Church, gave the address.

The service of institution took place under two large tents in front of the main academic buildings. More than seven hundred guests were in attendance. Among those were representatives of other seminaries and schools of theology, of other Episcopal seminaries, of other branches of the church, and of the American Association of Theological Schools, as well as bishops of the Episcopal Church and former deans of VTS.

Bishop Hines spoke of the school as "the second oldest seminary of the Episcopal Church" and of the installation of Dean Woods "at a time when theological education and the meaning of the ministry are fast becoming top priorities on both the agenda of the church and the world." He went on to say:

> The reason for this is increasingly transparent. For in a world where computers compute, and men stand on the moon, and human hearts are transplanted, and ABM systems are hotly debated, the question undergirding and overarching all these fabulous human achievements is the question of meaning. And the question of meaning is the question about God. And the question about God is the question about faith. . . .

Robert Sessum listened intently to the words of the Presiding Bishop. He and David had been asked to be crucifers for the gala outdoor event, since they were both from the Diocese of Tennessee. Following the service, Roy Green, who was the year's head waiter, supervised all of the activities at the reception, thankful that his two friends, "Duck" and John, had been willing to serve with him.

The Duck even hammed it up a little while pouring punch for the guests. Remembering a favorite film of his, *The Great Escape* (and more specifically the scene where Steve McQueen as a World War II American soldier in a German prisoner-of-war camp served moonshine at a July Fourth celebration), he repeated the actor's classic line: "Don't smoke right after you drink it."

But on a more serious note, David in his next article for *Ambo*, reflected on his history with the newly installed leader.

> Molle highly recommended that we go to our weekly forum hour one Tuesday last year, suggesting that if we didn't, we would probably regret it for the rest of our lives. That was the day Jesse Trotter officially announced his resignation, and Virginia Seminary began the search for a new dean.
>
> Since I'm from Tennessee, I was especially pleased to hear that the man chosen as successor to the throne was from Sewanee, fifty miles away from my home town of Chattanooga. But when I was told that man was Cecil Woods, something seemed familiar. And when we were first introduced last spring, we both stared at each other with that "I-recognize-that-name" look in our eyes. Well, over the summer I discovered that not only did this man once live in Chattanooga but when he was in college and I was knee-high to a duck, we lived across the street from each other.
>
> So I came back in the fall to greet an old acquaintance. And consequently, it meant a great deal for me to serve as crucifer at his installation, which the establishment happened to plan on my birthday.
>
> As I think back now to that first Tuesday when it all began, I realize how much I would have regretted not being there. For it was the beginning of a new era for this seminary, for Cecil Woods, and for all of us. And as we set out on this venture together, let me turn to a man I knew many years ago and say:
>
> Welcome to Virginia; welcome to a new role. Welcome, Dean.

On Wednesday, October 15th, the nation experienced an event described as the largest demonstration for a common cause in its history. People of all sorts and conditions participated in the Moratorium to End the War in Vietnam, and representatives from VTS—both faculty members and seminarians—were among them, offering their own prayerful plea for peace in Washington that day.

Some from VTS let their voices be heard; others did not. Many felt that participation in a demonstration was a potential violation of church and state, and that those preparing to enter the ministry should not engage in social action endeavors. Much discussion ensued on the hill that day about the pros and cons of such involvement, and debate continued on whether such activity was right or wrong or somewhere in the middle.

Among other topics, that subject was discussed at the home of the Sessums on the following weekend, as Robert and Donna hosted their new dean and his wife, as well as all of the Tennessee seminarians and their spouses. Fortunately for David, Patty had come up for the weekend, so he could share the occasion with his beloved. And it was a good opportunity for the new juniors to get better acquainted with their Tennessee kinsmen on a more personal level.

As before, one weekend was hardly enough time for Patty and David to spend together, and all too soon they parted once more, consoling themselves with the knowledge that Thanksgiving break was only a little more than a month away.

In that month, however, there were several occurrences that made their mark in the ongoing saga of our three central characters. Along with classes, field education continued quite smoothly for Bob, David, and John. They all enjoyed sharing with each other their ongoing experiences at St. Andrew's, St. George's, and St. Francis respectively.

But in late October, David had a problem with his field work supervisor. It was not Hedley, for that relationship was doing just fine. No, it was with Moody Burt, the assistant rector with whom David met on an every-other-week basis.

The two seemed to be in conflict over exactly what a supervisor should be and do. Moody felt that his role was simply to listen to the seminarian reflect on his experiences at St. George's, then ask him what he had learned. David felt that Moody ought to share more of what the ministry had taught him over the years. And after several sessions together, they were still at odds with one another.

Just what was the nature of supervision? Moody decided to present the stalemate they were facing at the regular group meeting of field work supervisors, a comparable element to the colloquies held for the seminarians. In the long run, the majority of those in attendance tended to agree with David's position and possibly the discussion had the result of elevating David in the eyes of some of his faculty.

Halloween arrived on a Friday, and Bruce Myers made arrangements to fly in some Maine lobsters for a dorm party. Everyone enjoyed the delicacy dipped in melted butter, at least until the next morning when the majority of the Wilmerites woke up sick. Nevertheless, they sincerely thanked Bruce for his generosity of spirit in wishing to treat everyone to a special dinner.

The senior class sponsored a big social event for the entire community on November 7th in spite of the fact that one of their classmates, Robert Sessum, had passed out at his field work site on Sunday. He stayed in the hospital for a week of tests but fortunately turned out to be all right.

More than four hundred people attended the dinner-dance at the opening of the new A.T. Mollegen Gymnasium. Of course there was time set aside during the evening to honor Molle and his wife. The building—a gift by one of Molle's classmates— had been constructed to recognize the years of service offered by Dr. and Mrs. Mollegen both to the Virginia Seminary and to the church at large.

The scheduling of that gala affair caused Bob, David, Ed, and John to move their monthly dinner and movie to Saturday, November 8th. They chose to eat at The Sirloin Room in the District, then go to see the film version of the musical *Paint Your Wagon* at the Apex Theater.

During the week of November 10th, Carl Cunningham and David Chamberlain served as sacristans. With Bob and Roy who had served the previous week, they joined the ranks of those who had completed the middler class requirement of chapel duty.

Chapel responsibilities included the following: seeing that all parts of the building were kept uncluttered by old leaflets and other paperwork, attending to proper distribution of prayer books and hymnals, posting numbers for chants and hymns, turning lights on and off, helping with communion preparation, assisting with the lighting and extinguishing of candles, ushering, taking up the offering, and doing anything else that might be needed in the conduct of a service.

As the first quarter drew to a close, David was able to purchase the common room's old television set for $25. (A new one had already replaced it.) Although it was not a color TV like Ed's, still the Tennessean looked forward to

having a source of visual entertainment in his room when
he got back from Thanksgiving break.

And with that in mind, David once again took to the
highway to spend the night in Roanoke, then head home
to Patty and his family.

CHAPTER 15

In the name of the Father, and of the Son, and of the Holy Spirit. Amen.

Sunday, December 7th, 1941, twenty-eight years ago today, the Japanese bombed Pearl Harbor. That was the beginning, the start of World War II for the United States. That's past history now, but we still remember it. And I think we remember it because it was the beginning. We tend to remember beginnings.

Advent means beginning, and it is the subject of Advent with which I wish to deal this morning. In order to do that, the first thing I need is a full definition of the term, and the logical place for that is, of course, a dictionary. So I looked up the word 'advent' and found three meanings. First, in a specific sense, it signifies the coming of Christ. Second, for the church, it represents the beginning of the liturgical year. And third, in a much more general way, it means a coming into place, view, or being—an arrival. In these three ways we see Advent as a beginning, and for me those three ways are quite closely connected.

First of all, let's talk about the person we worship. Specifically, Advent means the coming of Christ. Some two thousand years ago, a child was born in

Bethlehem of Judea—the Son of God, a Savior who was Christ the Lord. And His ministry was indeed an advent, for it inaugurated a new religion, a new era, a new hope for all mankind. The Holy Scriptures convey that message to us. And so we pray in today's collect for the Lord to 'grant that we may in such wise hear them, read, mark, learn, and inwardly digest them.'

Now let's talk about us, the congregation. 'Whatsoever things were written aforetime were written for our learning,' the epistle said earlier. And on this Sunday, we remember particularly the Holy Bible, the book that gives us the record of Christ. This Sunday comes in the church season of Advent, a season of four Sundays before Christmas, at which time we commemorate the coming of our Lord. Advent is a season of beginning for the church, for it is officially the beginning of our calendar year, and a time when we are called to rededicate ourselves to the service of God—in our pledges, in our time, in our worship, and in our daily lives.

Last of all, let's talk about me. The general meaning of advent suggests a coming into place or view—an arrival. And that meaning, vague as it may sound, describes me perfectly. Before you stands a twenty-three-year-old seminarian preaching his first sermon to the congregation of St. George's Episcopal Church. David Morrow Chamberlain is beginning his ministry. And although still a student—taking classes, doing field work, making preparations—he is beginning to find out what it is like to be on his own. No longer does he have the years of high school and college to choose what he wants to do for his life's work. And all too rapidly are going by the years of theological education that prepare him for that life choice. The time is imminent when he must go into the world and preach the gospel, to do that for which he is making ready.

And that frightens me. It frightens me because I can look back in my life and see the security that I've had. Whether from family, friends, or school, always before there has been that feeling of protection from the cold, cruel world. And now I have to face that cold, cruel world all alone. 'Men's hearts failing them for fear, and for looking after those things that are coming on the earth,' as the gospel said this morning.

But the gospel goes on. 'And then shall they see the Son of Man coming,' it says. I read that earlier in the service and that one line recaptures for me that sense of security. I find myself thinking back to the beliefs that have been instilled in me since childhood, and I find them more real than ever before. There is no need for me to face life all alone, for I put my trust and faith in someone beyond me, someone greater than myself, God. And in His name, life has a purpose and a joy I could not otherwise comprehend. Now I can go into the world and preach the gospel meaningfully, because it has meaning for me. I pray that it does for you as well.

So let me now tie together these three aspects of my sermon. Advent is a coming into place or view—an arrival. As a young man arrives at the beginning of his ministry, he discovers that the purpose of his life comes into view, for he has put his faith and trust in God. Advent is a season of the church year. And as we together begin a new liturgical cycle, I pray that together we might put our trust and faith in someone

beyond ourselves, someone greater than we are—God.
May our lives ever be an advent. May we always
share together a new life indwelled with purpose
and joy made possible by an advent two thousand
years ago—an advent, which continues to live today,
through Jesus Christ our Lord.

And now unto God the Father, God the Son, and
God the Holy Spirit, be ascribed as is most justly due,
all might, majesty, power, and dominion henceforth,
world without end. Amen.

David stepped down from the pulpit, and sighed with
relief. Incredibly, he had just preached his first sermon. It
was one of those moments that catches you up, when time
seems to stand still, when memories flood into your mind,
and when you know that you're at a milestone in your life.
It was what one might call an interlude.

As the celebration of Holy Communion continued, David
reflected on what he had said. He was only aware of one gram-
matical error made, saying the word "leer" once instead of "year."
But he immediately remembered what his father, a professional
sports announcer, had taught him about public speaking:

"Never go back; never correct yourself. You can't undo
what has already been done, so it's best to go on."

Several hours after having given his first sermon, the
Tennessean drove back to Wilmer Hall, wishing that family
and friends had been there to hear his first offering but
thankful at least for a tape recording. As St. George's most

recent preacher entered the welcoming gates of VTS, he was pleased that he had been able to quote in his homily the words that adorned the wall behind the altar in the chapel. Those were motivating words for all Christians to heed from the fifteenth verse of the sixteenth chapter of the gospel according to St. Mark:

"Go ye into all the world and preach the gospel. . . ."

It had snowed a little that Second Sunday of Advent, but it melted rapidly. David was soon back within the warm embrace of his room, now decorated with a newly painted side table, which he had brought back from home after Thanksgiving break.

After turning on some music and sitting down to rest, the resident of room #207 then took pen and paper in hand to write his beloved Patty.

And so, I have given my first sermon. I actually gave two, because I preached at both 8:00 and 10:00, though the earlier one was just a condensed version of the latter. It was quite personal, but the responses from the rector, the laity, and the critique committee with whom I met following the service were all positive.

I want you to know how very much your letter and your call meant to me this past weekend. But most of all, I want you to know how very much you mean to me. I feel that with you, I am beginning to discover what love is all about. And it's wonderful. And I did look at that front pew where you said you'd be in spirit.

Having concluded his epistle, David sat back in his chair and recalled the events of the last few days. A new quarter had begun, and grades from the first term were in. David was pleased that his overall average was a little higher than his normal "B." Courses for the second quarter would include Christology, the Epistle to the Romans, Medieval and Reformation Church History, plus homiletics.

Christology was to be taught by Molle, which of course made a lot of students happy. David was further elated to find that he would be with Dr. Reid for colloquy sessions. On top of all that, book costs only amounted to $25, and Tuesday and Thursday mornings both would be clear for sleeping late.

Needless to say, friends were happy to see one another again. Because their road trips were longer, and the vacation time short, Bob and John both had decided to stay on the hill and spend Thanksgiving together. Ed had traveled home for the break in order to spend time with his mother in West Virginia.

Before they knew it, the first Friday of December arrived, and it was time once again for dinner and a movie. Bruce Myers had recommended a particular spot to eat, so the regular four were more than happy to invite him along for the festivities.

Trader Vic's was a Polynesian delight, made even more so by the exotic drinks. The meal went along nicely until the final alcoholic beverage of the evening. It was called a "Scorpion," and the only detail all five diners remembered about it later was the straws that drained liquid out of a large bowl in the middle of the table.

The next recollection any one of them would have about the evening was sitting in the balcony of the Keith Theater with legs hanging over the railing as they happily watched planes fly by in a film called *Battle of Britain*. But by the next day they were back in the swing of things, and David presented his sermon to the dorm brethren, incorporating their constructive comments into his final draft.

Rising from his reflections of the past few days, the Tennessean walked his most recent letter to Patty over to the mailbox, daydreamed of seeing her at Christmas, and then returned to settle in for an afternoon nap. The Wilmerites dined in the refectory that evening, then returned to their desks for a few hours of study. The recent homilist had to admit that he found it much easier to concentrate on courses with his sermon behind him.

After everyone had said good night, David slumped onto his bed with a glass of cold milk and a couple of chocolate covered graham crackers to watch Channel 9's sign off from its broadcasting day. The station routinely gave a brief recap of the news before offering one of three thought-provoking closings—either a rendition of "The Star Spangled Banner," an ocean scene with instrumental music simply called "Meditation," or a resonant recitation of the poem "High Flight" by John Gillespie Magee Jr. accompanied by images of a jet plane careening through the sky. David thought it was a routinely pleasant way to end each day.

As was noted the year before, classes between Thanksgiving and Christmas were very few in number, so suddenly the colleagues found themselves with only two weeks left before the next break. But without a flu epidemic, at least there was more time to spend together than they had been able to enjoy twelve months earlier.

Bob, John, and Ed each had a chance to preach from the pulpits of their field work parishes, then the Ember Days arrived, requiring all to send seasonal reports to their bishops.

David began his letter by reflecting on events since his last epistle, specifically expressing his thanksgiving for his experiences at St. George's, as well as for the ongoing relationships he shared with friends in the dorm. It was becoming clearer and clearer to him that ministry was more about people than books.

Other than that, his thoughts turned to the future:

> With regard to the chaplaincy, I have received ecclesiastical endorsement from the Bishop of the Armed Forces, and I thank you for your participation and cooperation. I am now in the process of making final application to the army and securing a place for the introductory course at Fort Hamilton, New York, next summer.

For the last week of classes, everyone really got into the Christmas spirit, thankful for the celebration of a birth that was the very reason they were all at seminary in the first place. Out of that gratitude came a request to the faculty from a member of the junior class that Holy Communion be celebrated more than once a week. Bob was the first to endorse that recommendation, but he was not alone in supporting it. Meanwhile, another member of the junior class announced the formation of a prayer group, which would meet two nights a week in addition to the regular hall prayers in each dorm.

As serious as both the subjects of communion and prayer were, they were still supplemented by times of relaxation in the midst of study. One activity John and David enjoyed was taking time each weeknight to turn on the television for Johnny Carson's opening monologue. When they hadn't gone out for a late snack, the man from West Missouri often popped some corn for evening consumption. December 17th was one of those episodes they would long remember because in the middle of *The Tonight Show*, a wedding was performed.

Though it was not the most religious service ever celebrated, still for an entertainer called Tiny Tim and his bride known as "Miss Vicky," it was done with dignity and in good taste. Both of the future clergymen agreed—it came off quite reverently.

On Thursday night, December 18th, following chapel, the year 1969 culminated with a Christmas party in Scott Lounge for the entire seminary community. It was a wonderful opportunity to give thanks for the corporate family that God had called to live together in that place and time, through the gift of His Son and by the power of His Holy Spirit.

The following day all departed for home. David took off for Roanoke once again to pick up Patty, who flew in at 2:30 from Chattanooga by way of Knoxville for a fare of $44.10. They stayed together at the Travel Lodge, in separate rooms, for $12.66 apiece per night including tax. After dinner and a movie and some time together watching television, they kissed each other good night and slept soundly.

The trip home was a safe one, and they each celebrated Christmas with their families. Then the sweethearts reunited in Atlanta to spend a few nights in the home of Jeanne and Bill White, Patty's sister and her husband. While there, they enjoyed several dinner outings and three films. For them, it was an ideal way to say so long not only to 1969, but to the decade of the sixties as well.

CHAPTER 16

Yea, all of you be subject one to another, and be clothed with humility: for God resisteth the proud, and giveth grace to the humble.

That passage comes from the fifth chapter of First Peter, the epistle for the Third Sunday after Trinity. That is the text on which I have chosen to speak this afternoon. But I would like also to make reference to the parable of the lost sheep found in the fifteenth chapter of Luke, the gospel for Third Trinity, because for me there is a strong connection between the two.

When I first read the epistle, I was not sure quite what to do with it. I was only able to grasp a vague understanding of what was really meant by the terms 'proud' and 'humble.' Oh, I could give a general definition, I'm sure. I could talk of a prideful person as one wrapped up in himself. And I could speak of a humble person as one receptive and open to others. But that's about as far as I could go. To understand what the selection really meant, I had to dig somewhat deeper, both into scripture and into myself.

I find it quite easy to read scripture one time and think that I have grasped its meaning. But before I can really digest what is being said, I find it beneficial to try to relate what is being written about to an experience in my own life. So let me now try to define a sense of pride and humility that I have felt in my life, and from that, perhaps we can make sense of what is going on in the epistle.

I remember when I was in college. I had made my decision to go into the ministry. Now a lot of careful thought and preparation had gone into that decision and its consequences. And once I had made the decision and acted on it, I was quite proud of what I'd done. And I did do it. No one is going to tell me that anybody else typed all those letters for my bishop, for postulancy, for the various committees of the diocese, and for entrance into seminary.

The problem was that sometimes you can get so wrapped up in the materialistic aspect of things that you forget what you're really doing and why. You forget that the motivation behind your decision was based on a faith in God, a faith that had been taught to you—that had taken hold, grown, and developed inside you. And once you've gotten all that paperwork done and have been accepted, it's quite easy to sit back and listen to all the accolades from the people who have pride in you for what you're doing. And I tell you, I sat there and ate it up. I was quite proud of myself for the vocation I had chosen for myself. I was on my own.

I was on my own just like the sheep in Luke's parable. You see, when I looked closely at that sheep, it crossed my mind that perhaps he just didn't get lost blindly and dumbly. Probably he felt independent enough to strike out on his own for a while. So I imagine he wandered along for some time, absorbed in his newly discovered world. Then it hit him. He was lost. He had lost all contact with the world he used to know, and with anything or anybody familiar to him.

And I know quite well just what that feeling is like, because I remember when I left college, when I left behind all of the paperwork, all of the friends, and all of the people who had patted me on the back and told me how proud they were of me. I remember that drive from Chattanooga, Tennessee, to Alexandria, Virginia. I am sure it will remain in my mind throughout my entire life as one of the longest journeys, if not the longest, that I have ever taken. I had left behind the only world that I had ever known. Before me was the unknown. I was on a new adventure, and sadly I had to face the realization that I was all alone, or at least I felt that I was. The question that I had to ask myself was where had all of the paperwork and pride really gotten me?

So I arrived at VTS. I got out of my car and I looked around. I started to carry my bags into the dorm. And then someone extended his hand. I extended mine. A fellow seminarian and I had met. And BAM! There it was. I felt that I could give up that world that I had left behind. I could face my new life after all.

But I had to stop and realize why. Why did I feel that I could be at home here? It was not because I had done all that paperwork. It was not because I had come from Tennessee happily and proudly to start up on my own life with all those blessings from others. No, it was because a scared and lonely person had humbly crept into a new place and suddenly found himself accepted. Not accepted for what he'd done, what he'd been, or where he had come from. No, just accepted.

And it was a tremendous feeling—one of joy, satisfaction, and relief—rather like that sheep who had found himself lost and then found again. Not because he stumbled back on the herd. Not because of anything he had done for himself. But because he was found by the shepherd. And when the shepherd found him, he did not respond to the sheep because of what the sheep had done. He just accepted him joyously. Probably he picked up the sheep to carry him back to the flock. The sheep would have been swept off his feet by a saving act over which he had absolutely no control.

So now I look back at the epistle, and I begin to understand it better through an instance in my own life where I had been proud, where I had been humbled, and where I had been accepted through no act of my own. I had chosen a line of work, but I had lost sight of the reason why. My pride, my preparation, and myself had all gotten in the way of that greater something to which I was devoting my life. So at the very outset of my theological education, I was given an example of grace, a quality that lies at the very heart of our vocation.

'Yea, all of you be subject one to another, and be clothed with humility: for God resisteth the proud, and giveth grace to the humble.'

If God resists the proud, is it not because they shut themselves off from His grace, from others, and from the world in order to carry out their own affairs in life? Soon they discover that their work is of no use just in and of itself. A greater purpose is needed, a goal beyond ourselves, a goal that leads us to God. Through Christ, God has offered us grace by which to live, rather than having us struggle to live by works. To so great a gift we can only kneel in humble gratitude, and for our life's work, share that good news with our fellow man through the power of the Holy Spirit. Amen.

David preached that sermon to his homiletics class on January 8th. He had been thinking about it since driving back to the hill from Roanoke five days earlier. You might say that it was a testimonial to the way he had felt over a year earlier as he approached graduate school for the first time, a feeling that, safe to say, he no longer carried.

As 1970 dawned, a new decade was in the offing, and everybody at VTS hit the ground running. Bob, David, Ed, and John celebrated the new year with their monthly dinner and movie on January 9th, postponed once again from the first Friday since everyone had been traveling back from Christmas break the prior week. The Golden Parrot was chosen as the supper venue while the musical remake of *Goodbye, Mr. Chips* at the MacArthur Theater was their film choice.

On Monday, January 12th, David attended the annual parish meeting at St. George's. He was quite pleased to be applauded by the congregation for all that he had done in his work there thus far, as he approached the podium to make his report. As the heart of his comments, the staff seminarian made the following statement:

> The young people are at a time in their lives when they are coming out of set Sunday school classes and are facing adult membership in the church. They want an opportunity to talk, to express themselves, to be heard, and just to be. It is during this period of development that your parish leadership team has tried to provide them with a time for reflection on the experiences of their lives. In so doing, we have watched them share both feelings and events, and we've seen how they relate to their peers. Our ongoing hope is that what they have learned will give them further insight into the thought, purpose, and meaning of a Christian life, as well as how best to live it.

David sat down. He noticed he was quite anxious—not about what he had just said, for that seemed to have gone well. No, it was about what was going on back at Wilmer Hall. Ted Boswell would be graduating in May, and the election of a dorm proctor for the next year was being held that night. His friend John had been nominated.

The remainder of the evening at St. George's seemed to drag—not because David wasn't interested in everything that was going on in the parish but because he wanted to be a part of the action back on the hill. But not to worry, for when he did return to his home away from home, he found that John had, in fact, been elected.

The celebration afterwards, which took place at Lums, was followed in rapid succession by two other parties that week: first, a surprise for Roy after chapel on Thursday, January 15th, on the occasion of his twenty-fourth birthday, and second, the "Half Way Party" scheduled a couple of days later. Concerning the latter, David wrote the following article for the next edition of *Ambo*, while an icy wind blew outside, bringing temperatures down to as low as minus two degrees and snow, as deep as four inches.

On Saturday, January 17th, the middler class had a party celebrating the half way point of our seminary career. For me, it was not so much a time of pleasure and gaiety as it was a time of serious thought. As I stand now at this juncture, I find myself looking in two different directions: backward and forward. And I have to ask myself, Where am I? Where have I been? And where am I going?

When I came here in the fall of 1968, I expected much in the way of a graduate school, much in the way of books. And for a great part of my junior year, I faced that environment precisely. I was studying, and I was learning. But I had questions. I had doubts. I had difficulty seeing myself in the role of a minister. Surely there had to be more to all of this than books.

Now I look at seminary after a summer of clinical training, after five months of field work, and five months of colloquy. I look at seminary now having had some chance to work with people, and now the picture seems somewhat fuller. Now I seem to be doing, acting, and working with more purpose in my life.

Last year I sat behind books, and I asked myself, what will it be like when I go into the ministry? Now I feel that I have some knowledge, some idea of what my life's work will really be like.

Why is that? Why does it now make more sense? The answer, I believe, is because I am now working more and more with people. Now I am working with fellow human beings, and to me, that makes all the difference in the world because, to me, that is what the ministry is really all about—people.

As I go forward both with my preparation and into my ministry, I go with the realization that the most meaningful times in my experience here at seminary come when I sit up until 2:00 in the morning with friends, talking, sharing, searching, and finding what is meaningful to me and to them. It all really seems to come together here for me when we face with each other the problems and joys, the heaven and hell, of this very community in which we live—when we earnestly try to find meaning in what we are doing, to digest the gospel ourselves so that we may carry it forth.

Only in a personal way can the books and the clinical training and the field work and the colloquies have any real meaning. Only if we internalize and believe in what we are studying, doing, and striving for can we ever hope to go into the world and preach the gospel. Then and only then can we ever hope to be servants and witnesses to God, to man, and to our Lord and Savior Jesus Christ.

People. That was what the ministry was all about. God's people. Roy sensed that on Tuesday, January 20th, as he looked at all the folks who were seated that night in the refectory. As head waiter, he loved to supervise special dinners, and he usually secured the assistance of John and David to help him with the duties of the evening. The banquet for Phil Smith on that date was an event at which all three of them were happy to serve.

Everything went smoothly as a fitting prelude to the grand occasion of Phil's consecration on Wednesday, January 28th, at eight o'clock in the Washington National Cathedral.

"A congregation of approximately three thousand people was present, including hundreds of clergy," one of the seminary journals later reported. "It took three church choirs to get the chaplain elevated. They came from St. Paul's in Charlottesville, from St. Andrew's in Arlington, and from the Cathedral itself."

A few members of the VTS faculty took part in the service. Gordon Charlton, Director of Field Education, read the Evidence of Ordination, and Bennett Sims, Director for Continuing Education, read the Canonical Testimony. Both men had been members of the class of 1949 with Phil, and both were later to become bishops themselves.

The Reverends Bob Andrews, Ed Merrow, and Hedley Williams all served as marshals that night. Presiding Bishop John Hines preached the sermon. For those proceedings, the Wilmerites had a great view from the balcony.

Afterwards, our central characters had a late dinner at the same little restaurant in Georgetown where they had eaten together on their very first Saturday night in town. Jim Alby was with them for both the service and the meal and stayed up with them back at the dorm until the early hours of the morning reflecting on all that they had witnessed.

Then February was upon them. Dinner and a movie on Friday, the 6th, included great seafood at The Flagship on the waterway in the District, followed by watching Steve McQueen perform in *The Reivers* at the Annadale Theater in Northern Virginia.

The following Sunday had been tagged by the Episcopal Church for the annual Theological Education Offering, or TEO as it was succinctly called. Students from seminaries all across the country were asked to preach in various pulpits about their interaction with the gospel of Jesus Christ and their preparation for ministry. Prayerfully, the messages would result in contributions for support of the institutions committed to the field. David provided the 9:00 sermon for the Reverend Richard Stinson at Virginia's Fort Belvoir because he had been so helpful in assisting the chaplaincy aspirant with getting all of his paperwork together for the program the coming summer.

The next weekend was the annual college conference on the ministry and, happily for David, a chance to see Patty again. Arriving on Friday, February 13th, two days after Lent began and not at all an unlucky day as far as the Tennessean was concerned, Patty again planned to stay with Mil Ritchie in Arlington. She flew Eastern Airlines and got into National Airport about 8:00 at night. Having been met by her beloved, they were then able to enjoy one another's company for a couple of days. It snowed that weekend, but not enough to stop them from sharing a few meals and taking in at least one movie.

From that point, it was pretty much downhill to the end of the quarter. The resident of room #207 read from "The Gospel According to Peanuts" for his week of hall prayers, and soon started a new adult education course at St. George's focusing on the "generation gap," the widening chasm of opposing values and opinions between the older generation and the younger "Baby Boomers," who had been born after World War II.

Suddenly, the end of February and exam week were upon them all once again—not the best time for an annual visitation from the Bishop of Tennessee. Jack Vander Horst was his usual feisty self as he and his unmarried middler met for coffee at the local Hot Shoppes restaurant. Nevertheless, their conversation was very meaningful, as always. The candidate for Holy Orders brought his mentor up to date on all that had been going on, but there was one exchange between the two of them that David would never forget. It went as follows:

"I'm very happy overall in where I am at this point in my life," David said. "I'm glad I chose this vocation."

And the prelate responded with a gleam in his eye: "Don't ever forget—you didn't choose it."

The man from Chattanooga thought about that part of the conversation over and over again as he headed down the road to Roanoke on Friday, February 27th. It wasn't his own choice that had gotten him where he was. The very journey he had chosen was itself a gift of God, an opportunity to respond to the life, death, and resurrection of Jesus Christ through a call from the Holy Spirit.

That understanding gave David a renewed sense of both peace and purpose as he drove south the next day, unknowingly to see a cherished loved one for the very last time.

CHAPTER 17

The third quarter, which started on Monday, March 9th, had a most memorable beginning for the seminary community. Course assignments were interesting enough, at least as far as David was concerned. They were ethics, liturgics, a study of the Gospel of Matthew in Greek, and Theology of the Resurrection.

But what made the week memorable was the Conference on Racism, which took place on Tuesday, March 10th. David had been asked by a member of the faculty back in January to serve on a committee helping to plan the event and later found himself working in the areas of registration, hospitality, and arrangement of overnight accommodations for the out-of-town participants.

More specifically, David was to meet people in Scott Lounge upon arrival, take them to their quarters, then provide necessary information, resources, name tags, maps and diagrams, and also arrange coffee hours. All that went smoothly, but when the conference actually got under way, all hell broke loose.

Consensus on the hill beforehand was that the day would involve dialogue between members of the black and white communities and that a better understanding of the communication problem and ways to deal with it would emerge. But the opening comment by one of the invited speakers took everyone by surprise:

"I was hungry, and you formed a humanities club to discuss my hunger. Thank you."

It was clear that some members of the black community were tired of talking about the issue and wanted something done to alleviate the problem. But the way the concern was presented seemed to set an adversarial tone that was hard to overcome for the remainder of the day.

If anything at all happened on that Tuesday, it was that the whole matter was much too serious to solve with a conference. What had to be pursued was how best to rid everyone of fear, anxiety, frustration, and polarization, and to figure out how best to work together, to walk hand in hand together, to love together, and to live out the gospel together.

The Wilmerites wrestled with all of those "how best to" questions well past midnight on the eve of the conference. When the clock reached 1:00 in the morning, David thought it might be time to call it a night.

"Okay," Bob chimed in. "It's a night."

But the conversation continued for another hour. Obviously, the subject matter wasn't going to be dismissed. That was not only true for our central characters but for the entire seminary community as well. For the rest of the month letters passed, meetings convened, petitioners signed, and fevers raged until eventually two days of classes were called off so that the controversy could be aired.

During those two days of discussion, faculty and students not only talked together but also really began to communicate—to understand and minister to one another. By so doing, the burden of concern that everyone had been carrying finally came out into the open. There was hurt. There was sharing. There was love. There was unity. And that was good. None of it solved the problem of racism, but at least everyone on the hill became more aware of the elements involved in the controversy.

Meanwhile, life otherwise continued normally at VTS. On Friday, March 13th, David added a finishing touch to his room—a special pillowcase, embroidered by Patty with the name, "DUCK."

That night the members of the monthly dinner and film club ventured forth for their next outing, once again postponed from the first Friday of the month because everyone had been traveling back from spring break. The Embers was chosen as the supper venue and *Patton* at the Apex Theater as the film. But that was not the highlight of the day as far as David was concerned, for that moment occurred in his dorm room after returning for the evening. And what a moment it was.

Ever since he was a child, David had dreamed of owning his very own movie collection. His father, a sports announcer with a passion for music, had sparked the idea by his own fervor for collecting records. Pop, as David called him, owned one of the most impressive record collections in the country. Indeed, his personal collection of Guy Lombardo recordings exceeded even Lombardo's. David's father met the band leader initially when he was searching for one of his recordings so rare that even he didn't own it, and he was given Gus Chamberlain's name as the definitive collector. After he supplied it, the two men became friends. Lombardo had even invited the Chamberlains over to his brother's house once to watch a movie.

That fact piqued young David's interest in home collecting. Imagine seeing a movie in your own home! Ever since 1963, the movie lover had subscribed to a weekly periodical called *Boxoffice*, a trade magazine for the motion picture industry. It kept him up to date with the latest releases and all that was going on in the business of cinema.

David understood that film companies make a certain number of copies of their films to be circulated to theaters for "first run" showings. After those film canisters were returned to the company, most of the reels were junked, but a few salvagers bought some of them up and resold them to private individuals. (So long as copies weren't made and sold, the production companies apparently didn't care what became of the celluloid.) For years David held the secret desire to one day own a library of films, just like others might own a collection of books.

Earlier in the year, he had written to the *Boxoffice* editor asking for information about the actual purchase of prints of older films. A note came back, saying they knew nothing about such sales.

But several weeks later, a letter arrived from an organization called Auric Enterprises operating out of Kansas City, Missouri—the same city where *Boxoffice* was published. The company identified itself as one that dealt in the sale of salvage motion picture product—thirty- five-millimeter features available for purchase by individual collectors for private viewing with no copyright permission given to reproduce them or charge people for watching them.

David was thrilled. He decided to take a chance that everything was above board as far as the company was concerned. He wrote a check for $100 and mailed it to Auric to buy a selection from their available inventory. The item in question was a picture called *The High and the Mighty*, a John Wayne classic he had seen many times before, including at least once with his buddy John McCann and more than once with his father.

The week the third quarter began, Dot Bliss at the seminary post office notified David that two big boxes were waiting for him. David picked up what turned out to be nine shipping reels of film and hurried back to Wilmer Hall. Then he had to decide what to do with his purchase. The yellow pages informed him that there was a corporation in Georgetown called Wilmo that actually had a portable 35mm projector for rent. David placed a phone call to secure a reservation of the equipment for the weekend, and he extended the seminary community an invitation to a free showing on Saturday night.

On Friday afternoon, the 13th, Roy accompanied the new film collector on his drive over to Georgetown to rent the equipment and help him carry it back to the dorm. They loaded up two big blue cases in the back of the Volkswagen known as Sam, somehow managing to fit everything in, and then trekked back to the hill to unload.

That night, after their monthly dinner and film, John helped David set up the machine in room #207. They clamped in the first reel and started the projector running. When everything went off without a hitch, and the print was perceived to be in good condition, their cheers were loud enough to wake the sleeping all down the hall.

The same was true the following night in Packard-Laird Auditorium when the duo presented the film publicly. There were about fifty people in attendance, made up of faculty, students, spouses, and children. Everything ran smoothly. David and John developed a rhythm between them in changing the reels, which ran between fifteen and twenty minutes each. Thus, there was not too much continuity lost in the story even though the breaks came often.

The seminary community enjoyed the showing, a nice break from the tension caused by the racism conference a few days earlier. A voluntary offering was taken up to help offset the $57 rental fee of the projector, and since $53 of that was collected and John tossed in another $4, David got to see the first feature length film of his collection for free. Immediately he began to dream about buying another.

The Wilmerites got to see Peter, Paul, and Mary again just before Holy Week began on March 22nd, when all the middlers and seniors were busy with Palm Sunday services at their field work parishes. The annual married couples conference on the ministry had just concluded, coming in right on the heels of a two-day discussion on community and communication.

Maundy Thursday presented John with a new title. In addition to being proctor-elect, the dean designated him as the new doctor's aide, or dorm nurse, as it was sometimes called. It was a position designed for those on the hill to have a resource for any minor medical emergencies after hours that might need to be tended to in the absence of the resident physician.

David didn't need a nurse or physician, but that very night he was in need of an optician. After the weekly chapel service, he and John were invited to Bruce Myers' apartment for a nightcap. Bruce had gotten married over Christmas break and was anxious to welcome friends into his new home. While the Tennessean was sitting on the couch, one of his contacts popped out. No amount of searching brought success in retrieving the lens, so reluctantly the next day, the vision impaired middler had to fork over

$17.50 to purchase a substitute for the very first contact he had ever lost.

His frustration was short lived however, because on Good Friday, David had a nice treat. He received a phone call from a good friend and fraternity brother who was presently doing his initial military training exercises at Fort Belvoir. They both looked forward to getting together for dinner at the earliest possibility.

And as Holy Week came to an end, our central characters and their fellow dorm members were busy writing home with their latest news, along with some specific requests. Their baby pictures were needed for an upcoming display on the resident bulletin board. It was to be a "Who's Who" guessing contest entitled "The Little Men of Wilmer Hall."

Easter, the feast day of the Resurrection, arrived on March 29th, and as winter gave way to spring, so Christians everywhere acknowledged death giving way to life. The new film collector really did feel like a movie projectionist, running shows back to back, as he ended one service at St. George's, only to start another.

Tension from the Conference on Racism had finally eased, and courses were in full swing. Middlers were busy choosing special topics on which to report in their ethics class, and the man from Tennessee had settled on the subject of abortion.

After beginning his initial work on that project, David decided to use Thursday afternoon, April second, as a fitting time for a nap. But a knock on the door prevented him from drifting off to sleep. Expecting to see either Bob, John or Ed, if not Jim or Roy, he was startled to open the door and find Lance Workman standing there, his friend and fraternity brother who had called the week before.

Given the circumstances, David decided to skip the evening meal and weekly service on the hill in order to spend some quality time with his old comrade. They enjoyed a delightful dinner and conversation at The Three Thieves before Lance headed back to Fort Belvoir.

Hard as it was to believe, another month had gone by, and it was time once again for dinner and a movie. Friday evening, April 3rd, found the Wilmer Four at the Sakura Palace for supper then back at the MacArthur Theater for *Anne of the Thousand Days*. The theme of movies continued to color the next few days.

On Sunday, April 5th, Mr. Chamberlain preached his next sermon at St. George's on the topic of the Academy Award nominations for best picture of the year, appropriate since the Oscars were scheduled to be telecast the following Tuesday night. The theme was one of searching, how each of the five films expressed that concept, and how the church had always been the only true place where that kind of searching could find satisfaction.

Tuesday, April 7th, arrived as a cool and rainy day. David had just gotten Sam, his VW, back from its 24,000-mile checkup, and although he was about to need new tires, had no problem driving to The Village Inn that night to pick up a couple of pizzas for the Oscar telecast. The viewing took place in Ed's room, and the dorm members present were more than pleased to see John Wayne finally receive an award for best performance by an actor, winning with his portrayal of Rooster Cogburn in *True Grit*.

As the week progressed, John and David finalized plans for their next trip to New York at the end of the month, and Duck looked forward to Patty's arrival on the weekend of the 17th. The student body elected Don Wimberly as its president for the next year. And at the end of the week, the middlers looked forward to a class retreat at Peterkin Conference Center in West Virginia.

Friday afternoon came. With Ed having gone on ahead of the others, Bob, David, and John departed for the gathering. The trip over proved to be uneventful, but the arrival was not.

Ed met them with a solemn look on his face. There had been a phone call for David, and he was requested to call his mother at home as soon as possible. Apparently, there had been a death in the family. David walked with Ed to the reception area, expecting to hear that his grandfather was gone. But when he reached his mom on the phone, her tone was quite different than expected.

"David," she said with deep concern in her voice, "I want you to know that all my prayers and thoughts are with you at this time as I share some bad news. Honey . . . your father died."

After what seemed like an eternity, David was only able to respond with one word—"Pop?"

The voice on the other end of the line went on to explain the circumstances and details of an accidental death, initial plans and arrangements for the funeral, and other matters relevant to the heartbreak. The whole conversation probably took no more than ten minutes. Then wishing his mother love and prayers, the stunned student hung up and stood for a few seconds in silence.

When he emerged from the reception area into the sitting room, David found the assembled members of his class gathered as a congregation of support. Their comments ranged from questions about what had happened to offerings of condolences at such a time of great loss. David tried to respond to them as best as he could and then asked for the prayers of his classmates in the days ahead.

Having driven Flo over from seminary, Bob immediately volunteered to take his friend back to VTS so David could prepare for the trip home. John said that he would like to come along and would be honored to make any travel arrangements needed for the days ahead. Ed asked if he could go too.

The trip back to the hill was a hazy one as far as David could remember. He seemed to drift back and forth from present to past, from being in a car with brothers in Christ to being with his father at special moments in their lives together. David realized how glad he was that his dad knew that he had recently been able to purchase a copy of *The High and the Mighty*, the film that had meant so much to them in days gone by, and David hoped that Pop had been aware that John Wayne finally got his Oscar.

Once they were back in Wilmer Hall, the four comrades gathered in John's room. David was surprisingly calm in the midst of his personal storm. Discussion ensued among them about what they believed, what they felt, and how the two mingled together in a time of crisis.

"One thing I know," David said. "I will get to see my father again. He always taught me that as a Christian, you never have to say goodbye to someone, only so long."

When it was time to say good night, and after Bob and Ed had closed their doors, John and David as always offered a blessing to one another with the sign of the cross. But before the resident of room #207 could turn in, two more meaningful things happened.

First, there was a knock on the door. It was Dean Cecil Woods, there to offer a prayer not only for one of his students but also for a long time acquaintance. Their few moments together meant a great deal.

Second, as the dean departed, the Chattanoogan found

an envelope slipped under his door. It was from Ed, and the enclosed note read:

> David, it's rather quiet in my small square room this evening. A wispy breeze is coming through my window. As I sit here alone, I ponder over what took place this tragic afternoon. A message was given for me to relay to you. We walked together toward Peterkin's entrance hall. During that short brisk walk, I remember the finely worn gravel under my feet, then waiting in the parlor while news of 'Pop' was conveyed to you. I remember the long journey back home to seminary—no doubt the longest journey we shall travel together. In John's room, I vividly remember both words and tears as releases of inner hurt. And I realize how strong and how deep my concern is for you. I shall miss you sorely these next few days of painful testing by the Lord. Painful tears will be shed where you are going. Tears of sorrow will also be shed for you here. May God bless you, David, and your family. Your loving brother, Eddie.

With a change of planes scheduled in Knoxville and with Patty prepared to meet him at the airport in Chattanooga, David flew home the next day to bury his father.

CHAPTER 18

Five weeks ago my father died. I have witnessed many deaths in my life, but never before has the event of life's end fallen on someone so close to me. Death is a trying time. Death is an all-encompassing time. Many things are involved at the time of a death. There is the emotional response to the loss of a loved one. There is the practical response of arranging for caskets, flowers, funerals, grave sites, and memorials. There is the business response of handling the estate of the deceased, reading the will, distributing the property, and officially closing the door on the life of a human being. And perhaps the hardest response of all is to attempt the acceptance of life without that one person. Is not death always hardest for those who have to go on living?

This paper is done as a requirement for a specific seminary course. Ordinarily term papers either sum up the material dealt with in a course or delve into a certain aspect of that material. For a course dealing with the death and resurrection of Jesus Christ, it is sadly ironic that within its period of instruction came the death of one so close to me. And it is with the death of my father that I wish to deal in this paper. It will not be a paper of resources, summation, or in-depth study. It will be a paper of careful thought, reflection, and love. The passing of my father was one of the most profound and meaningful experiences of my life. And I think it only fitting that I devote my time, my effort, and my energy here, in order to pull together my thoughts about my father, myself, and my faith.

Pop was an interesting man. His love was sports, and being a sportscaster, he was an authority on what he loved. He and my mother had divorced when I was quite young, and Pop had been married and divorced twice since then. I always felt it tragic that he never found what he was looking for in a family. I lived with my mother, and I remember my childhood relationship with my father to be similar to that of a big brother, who took me places and did things with me. During college, however, I felt we both really came to know what it meant to be father and son. We could talk, share, and give of ourselves to each other. I have always considered it to be more than a misfortune that my mother and father were divorced, but I feel that in many ways it enabled me to come to know each of them as individuals, perhaps in a way not otherwise possible.

Pop had a strong faith. In the loneliness that he faced in his lifetime, I think that he really came to know his Lord. In the months before he died, there was no question that he was a man who had found something, who had come to believe in something, who wanted to share his belief, who wanted to give of himself. One could see that sense of giving in his dedication to his work, for it was a total involvement. He was constantly doing for others.

And now that man is gone. That fact is still hard for me to believe, hard for me to accept. It still seems impossible that that man, whose living faith was such an inspiration to me, is no more. He is dead! I cannot retrace all of the thoughts that have gone through my mind since that fact was made known to me. I can only say that it has been a bewildering feeling, a feeling of asking why he had to die, a feeling of remorse at his loss. But I guess most of all it has been a feeling of helplessness. Nothing has ever emphasized to me as much the pitiful state of man as has his utter lack of control over the one thing most vital to his existence, his own life. Never before have I felt so completely at a loss, so totally helpless. There was absolutely nothing that I could do, nothing that I could say that could possibly change the situation. All I could do was to accept it, to try to move on. And I found that feeling frustrating, indeed almost unbearable. And yet at the same time it was a profound feeling, one that forced me not only to accept and understand the death of my father but also my own limitations.

But in that state of loneliness, isolation, sorrow, frustration, and helplessness, I became aware of love. It was all around me. It was there at the middler class retreat at Peterkin, where I first received the news. It was there with close friends in the dorm the night before I flew home. It was there with my family. It was there with loved ones and friends. It was there at the funeral home and at the funeral. People from many varied places and many varied worlds had all come together in that one place for a common purpose. Over and over and over again I heard the words,

'I wish there were something I could do,' or 'if there's anything I can do, let me know.' But those words, no matter how many times I heard them, never got old. Each time I heard them, I felt a sharing, a strength, a love that I could not grasp by myself, that I could not grasp alone. Until that tragic experience happens in their own lives, those people will never know how much they did merely by being there.

It is again sadly ironic that the passing of my father came at this point in my life, almost two-thirds of the way through my seminary career, my academic preparation for the ministry. At a time when we are deep in the study of books, deep in the understanding of people, deep in the sharing of love, and deep in the turmoil of division, both within and without these seminary gates, I was struck with an event so profound, so meaningful, so shattering that is has brought everything that I have studied and believed directly to the surface. I was faced with death, the most threatening element of man's existence. But through the passing of one so close to me, I came to a better and fuller understanding of what our profession is all about.

That time comes in every man's life when he has to put down his books, step aside from his relationships, and take a good look at his life, his world, and himself. The death of my father was such a time for me, and if I had to single out one point that I learned from that experience, it would be the need for faith. At the time I received the news of that death, all of the books, all of my understanding of death, all of my intellectual arguments as to what death really was meant nothing at all. I myself could do nothing about it. I was helpless. And I prayed.

And in my own helplessness and in my prayer I was conscious of the love around me. And I gave thanks.

Throughout this quarter we have discussed the death and resurrection of our Lord and Savior Jesus Christ. We have spent time talking about the events themselves as well as the ramifications thereof. And, again ironically, we have spent time talking about the psychological effect that these events and circumstances had upon the disciples. I use the term ironic because through the events and circumstances that have happened to me recently, I can see that it is not necessary for the attitudes of the disciples to be based on empirical data, based on a photograph of the resurrected Christ, or based on their own intellectual understanding and comprehension of what had taken place.

After going through the event of my own father's death, with all of its emotions and responses, I have a much more realistic concept of what might have been the response of those first witnesses. Their response also was made after facing the event of a death and after realizing their own helplessness in the situation. Indeed, the events and circumstances surrounding them were quite profound and meaningful, and after the death of their master, they went through much soul searching. Perhaps it was then that God began to reach them. Perhaps it was then that they began to grasp hold of what really had happened. Perhaps then they came to see the great love that had been poured out for them and the great gift that had been given to them. Perhaps it was true of the disciples, as it was true of me, that there was only one possible response—a response in faith.

Where exactly does that faith lie? It certainly does not reside in man himself. We have already seen that man's attempt to understand, comprehend, or work with his own life situation is indeed a fruitless and futile one. Man is a helpless creature, and if he has any hope in a salvation, he must reach out to someone not bound by human limitations. He must reach out to someone not restrained by mortal existence. He must reach out to God.

Man's faith then lies in God. It lies in the promise of God himself. God has offered through the death and resurrection of his Son, our Lord and Savior Jesus Christ, a salvation for all mankind. Man cannot intellectualize that; he cannot rationalize it. He can only accept it. Man is faced with a love so overpowering that the problem of his own finiteness has been resolved.

And in that glorious promise man responds in faith, man responds in love, man responds in belief. And at a crucial time in my life, when I have been faced once again with that finiteness of man, I have found that my faith becomes stronger, my love more willing, my belief more sure.

My father believed in that promise. And you could see his faith living in him; you could see his love reaching out to others. He was a wonderful man. I loved him very much, and I shall never forget him. It's still hard to believe that he is gone, but I pray that I may be capable of giving the type of

love that he gave, of capturing the type of faith that
he had. And I pray that my father has found that
perfect peace and love made possible only by God,
through Jesus Christ our Lord. Amen.

David composed the above term paper entitled "A
Response in Faith" not long after his return to seminary
following the burial of his father, though it was not due
until a month or so later. Dr. Stanley, the instructor of his
systematic theology class, was to receive it favorably with
the following words: "The great truths of faith are indeed
tested and made our own in the crucible of suffering and
sorrow."

David's friends and fellow residents in Wilmer Hall
greeted his return to the hill lovingly and warmly. Though
it was not easy to get on with the normalcy and routine of
academic life, David personally found it both healing and
therapeutic.

Especially helpful and soothing were the audible
accents of life in the dorm, like listening to Bob's recordings of Beethoven's "Jesu, Joy of Man's Desiring," Mahler's
Eighth Symphony, Pachelbel's "Canon in D Major," and
Widor's "Toccata." Accompanying the music was often the
delightful aroma and percussion of John's late-night corn
popping.

David had an opportunity soon after his return to pay
a visit to Cecil Woods, whose own father had just suffered
a stroke. Though not happy for the reason, the Tennessean
was at least pleased that he could return a pastoral call on
a fellow resident of his home state, one who had meant so
much to him at the time of his father's death.

On April 15th, David had dinner with the Right Reverend
Arnold Lewis, Bishop of the Armed Forces, with whom he

had been communicating for some time. The elegant steak banquet took place at Fort McNair's officers club, and served as a good opportunity for the seminarian to focus on the summer session ahead.

On a not so serious note, along with his fellow hall residents, David signed a letter of protest to the powers that be, complaining about the noise that the air conditioner over at the new continuing education building was making. After all, it was depriving the dorm members (whose windows were open because there was no AC in Wilmer) from hearing Redmon's music in all of its glory.

On April 17th, much to her beloved's delight, Patty visited for the weekend. Arriving on Friday afternoon and departing on Sunday evening, she flew round trip on Eastern Airlines at a cost of $86.10. The couple spent their three days enjoying one another, reflecting on all that had happened the week before, and watching together for the first time *The High and the Mighty*.

The day Patty arrived was an important time in the country, for everyone had been watching the news for the fate of the crippled Apollo 13 flight, which fortunately managed to land safely on April 17th. April 22nd was the national celebration of the very first Earth Day, and when the 24th arrived, a certain two friends departed for their second trip to New York.

Bob drove them to Washington's Union Station on a rainy Friday afternoon. The traveling companions left on the 1:00 Metroliner, had a satisfying lunch on the train, and arrived in the Big Apple at about 4:00.

Having decided to try a new hotel, they checked into The Americana, unpacked, and relaxed a little before venturing out. Dinner was at Mamma Leone's, a wonderful Italian restaurant, but both Duck and John had trouble reading the menu since it was printed in the native tongue. The two ordered as best they could and were filling up nicely by finishing off what they thought was the entrée, only to find out that the main course had yet to arrive. Rolling their eyes at each other, the Manhattan returnees picked at their plates but soon had to acknowledge that "Mamma" had done them in. Hopefully, when they returned the next year, they could pace themselves better.

The middlers then went to see the musical *Man of La Mancha*. A Japanese actor portrayed Don Quixote. It was a little difficult getting through the accent at first, but in time the members of the audience acknowledged a powerful performance in a stirring presentation. The visitors closed out the evening with a brief sojourn in Times Square before returning to their room to watch Johnny Carson on television.

Saturday morning brought the indulgence of room service. David and John each had two eggs, bacon, toast, orange juice, and coffee at a cost of $6.57 apiece. They then took the subway followed by a ferry ride to the Statue of Liberty, made more special since it was the man from Missouri's first time there.

They ate lunch at an automat, a type of fast food restaurant where each á la carte item rested behind its own window in a wall of vending machines. From there, they were off to Radio City Music Hall to watch another movie. *Airport* was a satisfying action drama with some good performances in supporting roles, but as far as two particular viewers were concerned, it was not the excellent airplane disaster story that had uncoiled from nine reels of 35mm film stored back in room #207 of Wilmer Hall.

After resting a while back at the hotel, the pair dined at a Mexican restaurant called La Fonda del Sol, then took in another musical, *1776*, which both of them thoroughly enjoyed. Another visit to Times Square to see the lights of Broadway ended a most successful day.

Sunday morning presented another occasion for a room service breakfast before John and David attended one of the morning services at the Episcopal Cathedral of St. John the Divine. Following worship, the seminarians walked around the campus of Columbia University, where David's grandfather had completed his graduate study, then they grabbed a bite to eat while walking in Central Park.

They spent the afternoon visiting the Museum of Natural History and the Haydn Planetarium. Then, after retrieving their bags from the hotel, the travelers left for Penn Station to take the 5:00 Metroliner back to Washington. Bob picked them up in Flo about 8:00, and the trio returned to the hill.

With the exception of losing an hour's sleep on Saturday night because of daylight saving time, the weekend went just about as well as it could have gone. Both of the vacationers agreed that it had been a wonderful trip, and David found it to be an especially good respite from all he had faced back in Tennessee.

May arrived and with it the concluding few weeks of the academic year, as well as opportunities for suntans out on the roof of the archway connecting Wilmer to St. John's. On the first Friday, the Wilmerites chose their favorite restaurant, The Three Thieves, for their final dinner outing. The critically acclaimed film, *The Boys in the Band,* playing at the Janus Theater in the District closed out their movie-viewing season together.

Various events caused the next few days to pass quickly. On Saturday, an encore presentation of *The High and the Mighty* followed the student council spring picnic. On Sunday Mr. Chamberlain proudly watched several members of his youth group at St. George's present themselves to their bishop for confirmation. More and more, David was seeing that parish ministry might be a feasible option for his future after all.

Monday, May 4th, brought distressing national news. National guardsmen killed four students who were protesting the United States invasion of Cambodia at Kent State University in Ohio. David and Carl Cunningham, who were chapel sacristans again that week, were impressed by the number of individual and corporate prayer vigils offered on behalf of all those involved.

By the time Saturday, the 16th, arrived, various events celebrating the approaching end of the current academic year were happening all around. David attended the St. George's annual picnic and got a kick out of watching Hedley Williams at bat in the parish baseball game. And back on the hill, the yearly dorm picnic took place later that same day. Its highlight was the revelation of who was really who in the photos posted on the resident bulletin board, thus far simply identified as "The Little Men of Wilmer Hall."

The following Monday, the Tennessean had a call from Lance Workman, his fraternity brother with whom he had dined in April who had just completed his military training at Fort Belvoir. Unfortunately, their conversation was not a happy one. Lance had learned that Tom Matthews, a fellow fraternity brother, had been killed in Cambodia. David and Lance offered prayers on his behalf. The next day when David was elected president of the Student Aid Society for the following year, he accepted the position and responsibility gladly because it was not only a way of helping fellow students in need but also a way of honoring Tom and all those who had offered themselves, often even their very lives, in the service of others.

Then it was exam week once again, and naturally, Ember Day letters were due at the same time. The Right Reverend John Vander Horst was kind enough to respond quickly to one particular candidate's epistle, having just heard about the death of his dad. Touchingly, during his second year of seminary, Bishop Jack had also lost his own father.

The prelate went on to say how pleased he was to hear of David's election as Student Aid Society president, as well as his acceptance in the military chaplaincy program for the summer. And both the single seminarian and his mentor were pleased that Robert Sessum would be assigned to St. Paul's in Chattanooga following graduation.

As David read his letter from the diocesan office, he realized how incredible it was that another year had almost ended. It would be difficult to leave VTS again but good to get back home. Patty and he were already planning some time together, as well as with her parents in Biloxi, Mississippi. And after that, David was also looking forward in June to driving both his mother and his grandfather to North Carolina to visit family and friends for a few days.

David's final event for the year at St. George's was a youth retreat at Shrinemont, the camps and conference center of the Diocese of Virginia. Everyone enjoyed themselves but upon his return to the campus, the resident of room #207 was surprised to discover that there had been a major theft in Wilmer Hall.

Before the weekend began, a stranger had appeared who identified himself as a friend of the business manager and said that he would be staying for a few days in one of the empty dorm rooms—really the old continuing education room, which was not presently in use. Actually, the whole thing turned out to be a con job. The man was only there to "case the joint," as the media police would have termed it, and to find a time when people would be away so that he could access any unlocked rooms.

That he did on Sunday afternoon, John's 25th birthday. While lunch was being served in the refectory, the visitor made his rounds, getting away with what, again, the TV cops would call "easily fenceable loot." The Wilmerites returned to find a number of personal items missing from their residences.

David lost nothing, since he had locked his door when he left for the weekend (but then he always locked his door when he left for any reason anyway). John always locked his door too, except that once, and consequently lost his television set, as well as a few other things. As the weekend progressed, several of the seminarians later said that they had begun to become a little suspicious of the guy's presence, but not soon enough to do anything about it. Police, of course, were called in to investigate the scene, but nothing came of it. The stranger got away without a trace.

After that bit of upset, pre-commencement activities got under way. On Tuesday, May 26th, John and David once again assisted head waiter Roy with the retirement dinner of Clifford L. Stanley, MA, ThD. He was to officially step down at the end of the month, and, needless to say, the meal celebrating his life and ministry was a gala event.

On Wednesday, the 27th, commencement ceremonies began in earnest. As had been the case the year before, members of the junior class were asked to vacate the premises early so that single dorm rooms could be made available for visiting guests. The middler class, in turn, took charge of all graduation arrangements.

Bob directed the acquisition and distribution of academic gowns. David led the escorts—those who were asked to meet, greet, and take the trustees, speakers, and other special guests wherever they wanted to go. John took responsibility for the outdoor preparations—guarding the tent, making coffee available, and (in his capacity as doctor's aide) readying himself for any first aid emergencies.

The rehearsal went smoothly that afternoon, as did the missionary (baccalaureate) service and reception that evening. John was praying that the weather would be as nice on the following day and even petitioned members of the faculty for prayers of favorable skies but chuckled at their corporate response, which was that they were in sales, not management.

Thursday came with no significant clouds or problems. Jim Alby served as crucifer for the academic procession. Among those in line were ten seniors in business suits, who had refused to spend money on academic gowns. Their request was that a comparable amount be sent to the national church office for mission work, as well as to General Convention for a special program.

Ted Boswell, Robert Sessum, and Henry Witten were among the seniors who graduated. Three of those who had entered seminary in the fall of 1968 received Master of Arts in Religion degrees. The Right Reverend Phil Smith accepted an honorary Doctor of Divinity degree. And at the alumni meeting that afternoon, a portrait of Dean Jesse Trotter was unveiled for the seminary community.

And then it was all over; the Wilmer Four's second year of theological education had ended. Grades were in, and David was fairly pleased to see that he had made an "A" in ethics because of his paper on abortion; a "B" in systematic theology, thanks to the paper on his father; a "B" in liturgics; and, alas, a "C" in the study of St. Matthew's Gospel in its original Greek version. The field education line was once again positively marked with an "S" for satisfactory.

The next chore was packing up rooms for the summer. The film collector had been concerned for several weeks about the condition of the boxes in which his movie had originally been shipped. Wear and tear were beginning to show. He had driven over to the Wilmo Corporation in Georgetown to order three 35mm film shipping cans, the kind you see sitting in the lobby of a theater when a motion picture print arrives or departs. They would serve as perfect protection and storage for his possession, which would be locked up in his closet over the next three months.

On Friday, May 29th, the friends said "so long" for the summer, and David departed for Roanoke once again. Arriving in time to catch a show, he got his usual popcorn and coke, then started down a side aisle of the Terrace Theater. But he stopped dead in his tracks when he saw a poster in front of him advertising a coming attraction. MGM and Cinerama were re-releasing *How the West Was Won*. That was the first movie he and Patty had ever seen together, on the very night they met.

CHAPTER 19

Patty and David got to relive their first film experience together on June 8th in Birmingham, Alabama, of all places. They had stopped there for lunch and a matinée on their way to Biloxi to spend a few days with Patty's parents. That trip gave the two some precious time with each other and got them both back to Chattanooga in time to participate as members of the wedding party for the marriage of Janice Datres and Charlie Jones.

Hardly was David back from one venture before he was off on another, that time to accompany his mother and grandfather to North Carolina. Stops included Gastonia, Charlotte, Raleigh, Morehead City, and Atlantic Beach, giving the three travelers a chance to be a family again, as well as reconnect with other relatives.

Upon his return home, David found two very interesting pieces of mail. One was from Dean Woods announcing that the board of trustees had met and elected a new chaplain and associate dean, the thirty-nine-year-old Reverend Brice Sydney Sanders, then rector of Eastern Shore Chapel at Virginia Beach, Virginia. Sid was a younger brother of the Bishop Coadjutor of the Diocese of Tennessee, and had served the church in that state himself. He was a graduate of Episcopal Theological School in Cambridge, Massachusetts.

The dean closed his letter by saying how pleased he was not only with being able to make the announcement, but also with the decision of the directors in the first place. The entire seminary community was soon to find out that a wise choice had been made indeed.

The other letter waiting for David came from Auric Enterprises, announcing their most recent motion picture productions available for purchase. On the list was the classic of classics, *Gone With the Wind*, priced at $750. With eyes gleaming, David mailed a check that very afternoon.

On Sunday, July 5th, David flew to Newark, New Jersey to begin his basic course of instruction for the military chaplaincy. While lugging a very large bag to the cab stand at a time when luggage had no wheels, it did not take him long to realize the advantage of traveling with two medium-sized suitcases instead of one huge one. The taxi delivered the young second lieutenant to The Americana in Manhattan, the hotel where he had stayed with John in April. A good night's sleep helped to prepare him for his new adventure.

The next day, David took another cab to the United States Army Chaplain School at Fort Hamilton. As the driver crossed the East River and drove to the lower part of Brooklyn, the back seat passenger reviewed the pivotal events of his life that had brought him to that morning—six years of military school, four years of ROTC in college, a pinning ceremony confirming him as a commissioned officer, and a deferment for graduate school.

At 11:00 a.m. David's taxi rolled through the entrance
gates of his home-away-from-home for the next nine weeks.
Fort Hamilton was located on a beautiful site, just under the
Verrazano-Narrows Bridge, which marked the gateway to
New York Harbor and connected Brooklyn to Staten Island.
The suspension structure was especially beautiful at night
when the silky water below reflected its lights.

A military policeman instructed the man from Tennessee
to report to the bachelor officer quarters, or BOQ, for room
assignment. There he met his roommate, a Lutheran from
Iowa by the name of Gary Meador. Two others from down
the hall quickly introduced themselves, Mike Moore and
Bob Hutcherson, both Baptists from Texas.

The remainder of that Monday and all day Tuesday were
taken up with in-processing. The students were to receive
pay for salary, room, subsistence, travel, and uniforms, so
there was certainly nothing wrong with the income he'd be
receiving for what was technically defined as active duty
training.

The base was really a small city unto itself. There were
all sorts and conditions of stores, as well as places to eat,
a gymnasium, theater, laundry and dry cleaning facilities,
as well as an officers club, which fortunately had not only
a wonderful Sunday brunch but also a swimming pool for
recreation.

On Wednesday the opening ceremony took place followed
by a reception for the new chaplaincy candidates hosted by
the commandant. On Thursday things got under way in
earnest. The weekday schedule combined classroom work
each morning with military drill and physical training
reserved for the afternoon.

Courses centered on a number of different subjects.
Included were chaplaincy and ministry in the armed forces,

character guidance, pastoral counseling, military environment, support services, organization, and administration. Candidates had some homework, but generally evenings and weekends were their own.

Free time was not something that David, Gary, Mike, or Bob took lightly. Their very first night on base, for example, they checked out the subway system. The "RR Line" terminated at 95th Street in Brooklyn. That was only six blocks from the base, and it was clearly the cheapest and fastest way to get in and out of New York City.

Their first venture into Manhattan to see the lights of Times Square convinced the four new friends that they had indeed found a viable means of transportation. David especially was to find that his nine weeks in the area gave him ample time to discover the ins and outs of the metropolitan transit system.

His first attempt at exploration, however, came up a little short. On Saturday, July 11th, John and his mother were scheduled to come through New York on their way to Europe with a two-hour layover at Kennedy Airport. David planned to meet them at the airport for a visit and thought he had plenty of time to take in a show en route. Having seen the war film *Patton* just before he left Tennessee and given the military focus of his present circumstances, the movie buff decided that another action picture of the same genre might be in order. *Kelly's Heroes* was playing at the Loew's State II Theater on Broadway at 45th Street. After thoroughly enjoying the World War II caper, David made his way to the subway station to take the A train to Kennedy Airport. Trouble was, that line didn't go the entire distance.

David had figured that he could make the trip from Times Square in about an hour. But with the wait to use a bus transfer at the termination point for the subway, two hours wound up being needed to cover the route. The rising senior seminarians, therefore, had only a few moments to reconnect but looked forward to a longer visitation when the McCanns returned from their journey in three weeks.

While John and his mother were away, David continued to enjoy his new life on the army base. His comrades came from a variety of backgrounds. Some were in seminary, some were in parish ministry, some had prior military experience, some had none, but the program was a new experience for all of them.

There were four Episcopalians enrolled: Paul Gray, a middle-aged man who pastored in the local area; Dave Veal, who was at Sewanee with Bill Patten; Art Mack, a student at General Seminary; and David. All except Paul were rising seniors, and all but Chamberlain were married. Around the middle of the month, Art was kind enough to invite the other three over for a gathering at his seminary. David was happy to have the chance to visit that center of theological education once again.

David spent most of his time with his roommate and their two comrades from down the hall. Together, the four of them enjoyed seeing the sights of New York and simply walking up and down a few of the city's most famous streets—like Park, Madison, and Fifth Avenues.

The highlight of their time together occurred on Friday, July 24th. The second lieutenants arrived in Manhattan about 7:30 at night and immediately headed for the United Service Organizations, otherwise known as the USO. There they were able to show their identification cards and procure for free what would have been $11 orchestra seats for any available play. Their choice was *Purlie*, an 8:30 musical performance at the Broadway Theater on the corner of the

"Great White Way" and 53rd Street. It was a most entertaining evening.

The low point of their time together happened the following Sunday afternoon. They visited Coney Island and were
quite disappointed with how crowded, dirty, and smelly they
found the amusement park to be.

The four Episcopalians did have one more opportunity to
get together as a group. Bishop Lewis of the Armed Forces,
with whom David had already dined once, invited his chaplaincy candidates to a supper on Governors Island during
the last week of July. As in April, the evening meal was
both delicious and entertaining, and the time spent together,
informative.

But after almost a full month in the program, David
was beginning to feel more and more that what was being
taught in the classroom was merely a rehash of what he'd
already learned in ROTC at the University of Chattanooga.
In many ways the course seemed to be speaking to the
army's military structure alone, rather than to the chaplain's role within that structure. The irony for David was
that instead of enjoying what he thought were going to be
the religious aspects of the program, the Tennessean was
becoming more enlivened by the military facets of the daily
routine, such as leading the cadence chants in afternoon
exercise.

Letters from Patty and home continued to support him
during his time away, and he was quite pleased to learn that
Patty had been elected president of her hospital dorm. Also
in the mail were two large boxes from Kansas City. The new
film collector was delighted that his print of *Gone With the
Wind* had arrived safely.

On Saturday, August 1st, John and his mother
returned from their summer vacation in Europe. For that

occasion, David was at Kennedy Airport to meet them on time. As the three came into Manhattan by cab, the McCanns told the chaplaincy candidate all about their trip, and David in turn shared his experiences at Fort Hamilton thus far.

Getting away for part of a weekend was a real treat for David. The weather had been unbearable with smog and pollution hanging over the base for days on end with the humidity, oppressive. After having dinner and spending the night once again at The Americana, Sunday found the reunited trio visiting the United Nations, the Statue of Liberty, and Staten Island. As they parted company later in the afternoon, the two seminarians looked forward to their final year together at VTS.

As August progressed, David found himself eagerly anticipating the final week of his summer assignment. On the 23rd of the month, the chaplaincy candidates headed off to Fort Dix in New Jersey for some good old-fashioned fun and games in the field.

The activities were designed to give those enrolled in the program a taste of what it was like for soldiers to sustain themselves in a combat situation. David's most vivid memory of the week was crawling under barbed wire one night with live machine gun fire blazing overhead. The adrenaline rush completely calmed the throbbing headache he had suffered since morning.

The first few days of September were spent in out-processing, and at a little after noon on Friday, the 4th, the second lieutenants had become graduates of the basic chaplaincy course. Fond good-byes were said, especially to Mike and Bob, the Texas Baptists. Then David and Gary made their way to La Guardia Airport to check bags for later trips home.

Because their flights were not until early evening, the pair decided to go back into Manhattan for a film and final time together. They saw a picture called *You Can't Win 'Em All* at the Loew's State II Theater, where David had seen *Kelly's Heroes*. Afterwards, they made their farewells after an early dinner at the airport.

Gary departed first around 6:00, while David had to wait for another couple of hours. He took that time to walk around La Guardia and reflect on the pros and cons of his completed nine-week program.

David's flight did not leave the ground until after 9:00, and darkness was beginning to settle over the city. Twinkling lights from city buildings burned brightly. With skies clear and stars beginning to emerge, illumination from both above and below gave David the sensation that he was traveling through the galaxy. It was one of the most beautiful sights he had ever seen.

The final leg of the journey was a smooth one, and the plane touched down in Chattanooga around midnight. David was more than glad to see his girl waiting for him. It was good to be home again.

THE SENIOR YEAR

CHAPTER 20

Roanoke came quickly. All too suddenly it seemed, David found himself at his overnight stop on the route from Chattanooga to Alexandria. Since arriving home from New York, he had only been able to enjoy one weekend with Patty, family, and friends before departing again. On Labor Day Monday, September 7th, he checked into the Travel Lodge once more.

Chisum was playing at the Terrace Theater. David always enjoyed a good John Wayne film, and that one was better than average. He couldn't help but wonder how his father would have liked it. After consuming a late cheeseburger from the hotel restaurant, he turned in for the night.

Tuesday's sun ascended, but David was not ready to rise with it. Sleeping in until late morning, he was still able to eat, hit the road, and arrive back at the seminary by around four o'clock in the afternoon. That gave the Tennessean time to unpack before attending the annual "Well, Here I Am" picnic scheduled for 5:30 in front of the refectory.

Bob, David, and John reunited at the early evening affair and soon realized just how much had happened during the summer months. Of course, John and Duck were fairly well up to date with each other's experiences, but they hadn't heard much from Bob. He had spent his last twelve weeks working in the Northern Virginia area, both at St. Andrew's on spiritual matters and at VTS painting "No Parking" on the curb around the campus quadrangle.

Beyond the constellation of the three of them, several other significant events had taken place over the summer. First, Roy Green had gotten married on the 29th of August, so he was no longer an eligible bachelor on the hill. Second, Bruce Myers had decided not to return for his last year, so he and his wife would be staying in Maine. And third, Carl Cunningham had recently lost his father. The two now-senior seminarians from the Diocese of Tennessee had both buried their dads within the same year.

But most surprising of all was the fact that Ed Mullins had moved out of Wilmer and into Madison Hall. David was shocked to hear that news from another dorm resident. When asked the reason why, the man from West Virginia had only said that he felt it was time for a change. At the risk of being egocentric, David could not help but wonder if something that he had done or said had caused his friend's move—or perhaps something that he had not done or said, like not responding as gratefully as he could have to Ed's heartfelt letter when Pop died.

At dinner, Bob and John confessed that when the two of them heard the news, they too had wrestled with questions and possible answers for Ed's departure. Maybe they had not been as inclusive as they could have been in their various outings. Perhaps it was something else altogether, but the bottom line was that so far, their pockets were lined only with guesses. Unless Mr. Mullins chose to share more, those who had lived with him would never have a full explanation, only suspicions and hurt feelings.

That night, further unpacking and initial reconstruction of rooms was interspersed with greeting both old and new residents of the dorm. David disappeared from the premises early to spend some time with Carl Cunningham, reminiscing about their fathers. As meaningful as their visit was, it also proved to be an emotionally draining experience, so David returned to the seminary quite tired. He only had enough energy to play his banjo (the one Carl had lent him) for a little while before he drifted off to sleep.

Wednesday, September 9th, found David up for breakfast early as usual so that he could nap for a few moments before continuing with the rest of the daily schedule. But on that particular morning, an experience occurred that the Tennessee bachelor and senior seminarian thoroughly enjoyed. It was customary for one of those in attendance at the first meal of the day to give the blessing. The privilege fell that time to a member of St. John's Hall who offered the following petition:

> May the Lord bless us and bind us,
> And tie our hands behind us,
> And throw us in the bushes,
> Where the Devil can't find us. Amen.

That offering got those sitting in the refectory happily through the next few hours of their Wednesday, which included both the business and the mechanics of starting another academic quarter. At 9:20 a.m. checks were written to pay bills for tuition. At 10:30 a coffee break allowed everyone the opportunity to visit, and that was followed by class registration in Packard-Laird Auditorium an hour later.

David was pleased with the fall portion of his curriculum, which consisted of a second round in homiletics, another course in systematic theology, a class in Christian education for the parish, and a study of the Epistle to the Galatians

in Greek. Most lectures were to take place in the morning, which again would offer David the opportunity for free
afternoons. His field work, of course, was set to continue at
St. George's.

After lunch, the single men resumed the task of getting
their living quarters back into shape for the year. David
had a fairly efficient system for his place, so he was done
quickly. But he had one thing left to do.

There were two boxes sitting on the floor with what
amounted to thirteen reels of 35mm film in them. *Gone
With the Wind* needed to be dealt with. Fortunately, there
was enough time left in the afternoon for a drive over to
the Wilmo Corporation in Georgetown to order three large
shipping cans for storage. With that done, the new senior
arrived back on the hill only to find another letter from
Auric Enterprises in Kansas City. On their latest list was
How the West Was Won, priced at $350. Because that film
was so special to Patty and him, he wasted no time in dis-
patching a check.

The dinner menu was not too exciting, so Bob, David, and
John decided to venture out after hall prayers to visit their
favorite evening haunt, The Village Inn. Over the summer,
all three of them had missed the pizza, the beer, and that
tasty blue cheese dressing they always found on a cold tossed
salad. The friends stayed a little longer than usual that
night, enjoying the fellowship of one another's company,
reflecting further on their summers, and then looking ahead
to their last year of school, their last year of institutional
theological education, and their last year together. For the
present though, they enjoyed being home again.

Thursday, September 10th, classes began, culminating at
7:30 that evening with the celebration of Holy Communion,
which served as the first corporate worship experience of the

year for the entire seminary community. Dean Cecil Woods preached, and the new chaplain presided at the altar. Due to a past bout with throat cancer, Sid Sanders had a raspy quivering voice, but one that was full of compassion and feeling. He would soon be one of the most beloved members of the faculty.

John took up the collection. David brought up the bread and wine. All gathered at the African rosewood railing as an offering of themselves to the Lord of life, who had already offered Himself to them in the breaking of His body and the shedding of His blood. As consecrated elements were received that night, the Wilmerites once again were reminded they were back home.

Next day was Friday and time for the monthly dinner and a movie group outing. The attendees felt the absence of Ed Mullins sharply, but all they knew to do was to give him the courtesy of honoring his wishes. Jim Alby quite naturally filled the void on that evening, and he even christened the party by bestowing it with a title. For some time, the residents of Wilmer Hall had been trying to come up with an appropriate name for their foursome. The closest they had gotten was "Epicureans," but that sounded too lofty. Jim had the perfect modification, combining that aforementioned term with an Anglican twist. So, the "Episcureans" dined at The Three Thieves, then watched *Catch 22* at the Cinema Theater, not far away.

On Saturday the 12th, David gave part of the annual orientation to the junior class, serving in his capacity as president of the Student Aid Society. He was subsequently pleased with the success of the voluntary fund drive. Also being senior editor of *Ambo* and a member of the selection committee for the class gift, the Tennessean felt that he had plenty on his plate in the way of extracurricular activities—more than enough to occupy his time when he was not studying or socializing.

Hedley phoned that Saturday afternoon about field work beginning the next day, a call that David received happily. He had really missed St. George's over the summer, especially the kids, and he was becoming more and more convinced that parish ministry really was what he wanted to do after all. Sunday, September 13th, a grand reunion took place in the parish hall and an even larger one at the House of Pancakes following the morning services, as the young people gathered with their returning advisor.

David was looking forward to his responsibilities for the fall: a chapel service for the preschoolers, a confirmation class for students in the seventh grade, a youth group program on Sunday evenings, and an occasional sermon, plus, of course, participating in church services on a regular basis. And already he was at work on an agenda for the Episcopal Young Churchmen, or EYC, and their retreat coming up the third weekend in October.

Monday . . . Tuesday . . . Wednesday . . . Thursday . . . Friday . . . Saturday . . . Sunday. Suddenly David realized, as he returned to the hill later in the day, that one full week of his senior year had already passed.

John was delighted. After two years of disappointment, he finally found his name listed in the class roster section of the annual seminary catalog. As he completed painting his room in Wilmer Hall, he felt happy to know that finally the longstanding clerical oversight had been corrected.

Duck picked up another package from the post office. Instead of 35mm film reels, that box contained the new stereo unit he had bought before leaving Fort Hamilton. Hooking it up to the tape deck already installed in his living quarters, the resident of room #207 discovered that he had created an atmosphere of quadraphonic sound most pleasing to the ear.

Bob continued to enjoy working in the library. It not only gave him an activity to complement his studies but also generated some income for the purchase of a new classical record or two every now and then. He still loved to listen to music, as did his parakeet companion, Jigger.

With the first full week under their belts, the three class-mates headed full steam into the fall quarter. The routine of academic discipline seemed to return quickly, and before they knew it, Thursday night brought another corporate celebration of Holy Communion, or Eucharist, as it was becoming more commonly known. Molle preached that evening, so certainly everyone was inspired.

On Friday, September 18th, there was a party given for Roy Green and his new bride. Single friends on campus were anxious to meet Gail and to chip in for the gift of a coffee and tea set. It was a good time for one and all.

As the second week of his senior year concluded, David wrote to Patty, as well as to his mother and grandfather. To all three of them he expressed thanks for the trips they had shared that past summer, then brought them up to date as follows: "The year started off quite success-fully. After last year's third quarter of unrest, dissension, and question, we began this term with a renewed sense of optimism and purpose in our work. My ongoing prayer is that it continues."

As the month progressed, humidity seemed to be even
crueler than David had experienced in New York, but otherwise, the next couple of weeks brought no specific concerns.
David prepared to write his initial article for the year as
senior editor of *Ambo*.

The term "senior editor" sounded more prestigious than
it was. The title simply referred to one who was responsible
for collecting information about his particular class. Thus,
there was also a "middler editor" and a "junior editor," but
the task was taken no less seriously. The following article
entitled "Rebirth" soon appeared:

> After several days of planning and building,
> I finally got my room in Wilmer Hall back in some
> semblance of order. Having done so, I sat down
> to write a few people and inform them that I was
> alive and well in Virginia, ready to begin my final
> year. It was while reflecting on the first few days
> of the current academic term, that I found myself
> also thinking back to the events that took place
> in the spring of last year and comparing them
> with now.
>
> Those of us who were here will remember (and
> those of us who weren't probably have heard) that
> the third quarter of 1969–70 was 'interesting' to say
> the least. It was a time when a lot of things came
> to a head, and a time when a lot of things came
> into question—the Conference on Racism, faculty
> recommendations, certain classes. Whether it could
> be defined as spring fever, fear, anger, lack of trust,
> or something else, it was a time deemed important
> enough by both faculty and students to sit down, talk,
> share, and communicate. Some felt encouraged. Some

felt discouraged. But as is life, regardless of what is felt, things move on.

Now we come together once again. I'm not sure exactly what happens in the summer. Maybe it's just that a time is needed to think, to get away from it all, to do something else. Maybe it's that when we return, the community has changed. Some have not come back. And among us there is some 'new blood' as the saying goes. Maybe it's merely the fact that a new year has begun. And because of that, we begin anew. We undergo a sort of rebirth.

Whatever it is, I have noticed since we returned an optimism and purpose that I haven't seen in a long time. The administration has reemphasized the goals, the rules, and the concepts of just what it means to be here. The students—regardless of whether it be in chapel, class work, field work, or colloquy—have no doubt that we have 'started' once again.

So at this new beginning, let me suggest to both faculty and students that we start hand in hand. Let me suggest that we look at this world of theological education together, sharing our joys and our frustrations, our happiness and our sorrow, our successes and our failures. We have a dean, a chaplain, a faculty, and a student body willing to learn. I pray that we might be able to do so with one another. And by so doing, hopefully we will engage in an ongoing renewal of our faith, our hope, our trust, our very Christian lives. Perhaps the right word to use in summation is one that I used earlier—rebirth. After all, that's a great deal of what the whole Christian enterprise is all about.

CHAPTER 21

O
ctober began with three social outings in a row for John and David. On Thursday, the 1st, they were invited over to Bambi and Ken Henry's place to watch Johnny Carson's tenth anniversary celebration of his hosting *The Tonight Show*. The four of them had a good chance to visit with one another, as well as see the program.

Friday evening, the 2nd, the four Episcureans dined at Hogate's, another seafood restaurant on the District waterway, very close to The Flagship, where the group had eaten the previous February. David consumed the largest flounder that night he had ever seen. Later, as was their custom, they took in a movie—one called *Getting Straight*.

And having rented the 35mm portable projector again from Wilmo, John and David presented *Gone With the Wind* to the seminary community on Saturday evening, the 3rd. That exercise was designed as another opportunity for both faculty and students to enjoy some entertainment and recreation time together, and it proved successful in every way, even with the feature running over four hours because of reel changes.

The next day David preached once again at St. George's, though his World Communion Sunday sermon was basically a reflection on his summer program in New York. The comments that he received in the parish hall following the services were most interesting, two of which stood out. First, Hedley told him that his own first church assignment had been only one block away from Fort Hamilton, certainly a meaningful coincidence. Second, a member of the congregation posed an intriguing question to the future chaplain:

"How do you rationalize being a man of God and, at the same time, part of a system structured for war?"

The senior staff seminarian thought for a moment, then replied as if he had rehearsed his rebuttal.

> No matter in what kind of sinful context men of God are placed, they are still needed— needed by the world, needed by God's people, and certainly needed by the men and women of the armed forces, who both serve us here and fight for our country far away from home. They are a very important part of the reason why in our own liturgy we pray for the whole state of Christ's Church and the world.

The reply seemed to satisfy the parishioner, who after expressing his appreciation, moved on to visit with someone else. David stayed at coffee hour for a little while longer before adjourning to IHOP with the young people. Then, following another satisfying brunch and discussion with the kids, he headed back to the hill for an afternoon nap.

Dinner at the refectory brought another opportunity for interaction among the single students. After almost a month of courses, names and faces were finally beginning to click for the newcomers, and the older members of the VTS family were trying to personally acknowledge newer classmates as well.

Bob Appleyard, Percy Brown, Bob Cummings, Jay Hobbs, Sam Mason, and Steve Park were a few of the faces that made up the middler and junior class members who resided in Wilmer Hall. But it was a couple of additional folks who became principal players in an event that took place at the dorm in early October.

Geoff Price and Dave Upton roomed next to each other just across the hall from the Chamberlain residence. Geoff was known for taking extremely long showers—two hours in length sometimes, as hard as it might be to imagine. That fact was not appreciated by other residents of the second floor, who often had to wait in line for the remaining stall in their common bathroom.

So, one night Price departed his room for another bathing session. He never locked his door, so Upton felt it to be a perfect time for seminarian revenge on the Wilmer water waster. As soon as he heard the water running, the next-door neighbor hurried into Geoff's room, grabbed his keys, locked the door, disappeared back into his own abode, locked himself in, and waited.

After what seemed like an eternity, the shower stopped. Having dried himself, Price emerged from the bathroom and walked back down the hall toward his room whistling. The whistling stopped, however, when the door knob did not yield submissively to the turn of his hand.

Having no doubt what had happened, and without a moment's hesitation, the newly washed student walked directly to the room next door. At louder than normal volume, he raised the question:

"Upton, did you lock me out of my room?"

All that Price heard from within was snickering. He began to knock.

"Upton, have you got my keys?"

No response. The knocking got louder.

"Upton. Give me my keys."

Still no response. Price began kicking the door. By that time, Bob, David, and others on the floor had gotten up to close their doors so they could resume study in some semblance of silence.

"Upton, give me my damn keys."

Again no response. The kicking and the banging on the door got louder and louder.

"Upton . . ."

"What the hell is going on down there?" came the voice of John McCann, the proctor, as he emerged from room #204. "Price, how do you expect anybody to get anything done around here with you making all of that noise?"

The locked out seminarian tried to explain the situation as John approached then passed on by him to knock on the room next door.

"Upton, have you got Price's keys?"

The door opened, and Upton sheepishly handed over the solicited item to its fuming owner, although a little snickering was still detected. Each of the miscreants then quietly retreated to his own space. McCann walked back down the hall but not without a few additional words:

"Now see if you two children can't play a little quieter, after all this is a theological graduate school, not a nursery. Good grief."

The door to #204 slammed shut. Silence followed. You could have heard the proverbial pin drop.

About five minutes later, David heard some footsteps, then a gentle tap on the outside of his door. He opened it to find the man from West Missouri standing there.

"Well," he said, "did I sound authoritative?"

"No," Bob Redmon uttered as he came up behind him. "Just mad."

The three friends laughed together. The entire incident

had been an interesting stress reliever in the midst of a hectic week. Juniors were busy studying for upcoming biblical content quizzes. Middlers were trying to figure out how to balance the academic load with field work requirements, and seniors seemed to be forever writing sermons.

That very night of the shower episode, John was searching for a topic on which to preach.

"I'm getting a little worried," he confessed to his comrades. "I can't think of a thing to talk about."

"Why don't you write a sermon on that?" David suggested.

"Good idea," Bob chimed in.

They looked at each other for a minute then parted company to resume study. John took the idea and ran with it. He built his sermon for homiletics class around the very fact that he couldn't think of anything to say. The point was then made that his salvation was not based on how good a message he preached, or even how successful a minister he might become. Salvation was based solely on the grace of God through Jesus Christ. His presentation was awarded an "A."

The weekend arrived, bringing with it David's 24th birthday. Patty arrived on Friday afternoon and stayed until late Sunday, boarding again with Mil Ritchie in Arlington. That first evening Patty and David spent together, they watched *Gone With the Wind*. Saturday night in honor of David's birthday, Gail and Roy Green joined them for dinner at The Three Thieves followed by the movie *Tora, Tora, Tora* at the Uptown Cinerama Theater.

In addition to delivering presents from home, Patty gave David his first ecclesiastical stole, one that she had lovingly stitched herself. Roy presented David with a much needed tie, and Bob and Jim both had found fitting cards.

For the second year in a row, John had to miss David's birthday celebration because of a youth retreat at Shrinemont with his kids from field work. But he left a note with a piece of tape stuck to it. On the tape he had written "35mm," and the accompanying note read as follows:

> Happy Birthday and many happy returns of the day. Since the available greeting cards didn't say what I wanted, I figured I'd just have to say it myself. The tape below represents a roll of 35 mm splicing tape, at least as far as the Wilmo Corporation is concerned. All you have to do is walk in and pick it up when it arrives.
>
> All kinds of good feelings are associated with the movies. It's been my great joy and thrill to be able— thanks to you—to share the fun, entertainment, and good times together that they have brought. I suppose I could launch into a lot of homiletical analogies about splicing tape sealing both film stock and relationships, but instead I will just say again 'Happy Birthday.'

He signed the message simply, "Brother John."

Cooler weather prevailed for the latter part of October. Windows formerly opened to capture cooler breezes, were being shut to the elements, yet the closed windows did not shut out the glorious colors of autumn that encircled them. As the month progressed, letters came in from friends of days gone by. Ted Boswell had written, asking how everyone was, and so did Bruce Myers. And Robert Sessum had sent for review purposes a copy of the previous year's canonicals, the exit examinations that seniors were required to take after graduation.

David was not ready to start studying for those tests yet, however, for he was busy getting ready for a youth retreat with his own field work kids at Shrinemont the weekend of October 16–18. The subject for their time together was "values," but David was to find himself not so much intrigued by the theme as by watching his young charges both plan and execute all aspects of the forty-eight hour period. From organizing and leading discussion groups to setting up and enforcing rules of conduct, David was pleased at how they carried it all off. The senior staff seminarian was later to write Patty:

> I think it was educational as well as interesting for them to realize both the benefit and the frustration of leadership, not to mention the responsibility. I do hope that they will be able to take what was learned and build on it for future events.

The soon-to-be adult members of St. George's did not disappoint their mentor. At a later Sunday evening session, they planned activities for every meeting that remained in the year.

Back in Wilmer Hall, John had been busy scheduling his own series of events. As proctor, he wanted to enhance dorm life somehow and thought a good way to do that might be by inviting faculty members to join his fellow residents for nightly hall prayers.

Several weeks earlier, the dean had accepted an initial invitation. He arrived at ten o'clock on the appointed night for worship and discussion and stayed until after midnight to discuss seminary, theological education in general, and the ministry. His sharing made for a most meaningful experience.

Other guests soon followed. The resident seminarians enjoyed especially the company and presence of Albert Mollegen, Sid Sanders, and Cliff Stanley. Thus there was more and more time spent with faculty members outside of the classroom, not only at hall prayers and the Thursday night corporate service but also at open houses in the homes of the professors themselves, specifically the special event of afternoon tea with Dr. Reid.

The last full week of the month arrived, marked by a few notable occurrences. David and John had discovered a new pastime for Saturday night late show viewing. The old Charlie Chan mystery movies proved to be an excellent excuse for takeout pizza from The Village Inn.

The World Series prompted, for David, fond memories of his dad. Driving his car back from its 30,000-mile checkup at the local Volkswagen dealership one afternoon while listening to a game on his AM radio, the Tennessean drifted back in time to childhood summer days when the crack of the bat and the organ crescendos of broadcast games were his constant companions around the house. He sure did miss Pop.

Speaking of sports, October 30th was quite a special day for the man from West Missouri. The seminary calendar, much to his surprise, named that Friday as "John McCann Day." John had been officiating for VTS student football games all three years of his life on the hill. His teams had gotten together early during their third season to plan a way of thanking him for the hard work and effort he had rendered. As the community gathered for lunch on the aforementioned date, they set aside a moment for a special presentation.

Recognizing John's effort, they gave him a commemorative referee's shirt and an engraved whistle—which he promised not to blow in the refectory. It was obvious that all the acknowledgment meant a great deal to John. For the gifts and affection offered, he was later to write a note of appreciation in *Ambo* entitled "Whistle Stop."

> I want to say thanks again to the junior, middler, and senior football teams and everyone else involved for the gift of the zebra shirt and the engraved whistle presented to me last Friday. Thanks also for the gifts of joy, warmth, and pleasure those gifts brought and will continue to bring.
>
> I've had a lot of fun officiating the past three years, and though at times during games I felt that the players thought I possessed the betrayal qualities of the twelfth disciple (and probably hoped his fate would befall me— perhaps immediately after the game), still it's been rewarding, but no more so than it was on that Friday.

The epistle was signed simply with the Jewish word for peace, "Shalom."

Halloween arrived the next day, and while taking a break in his ongoing taping endeavors of favorite music, David sat down to write letters home to both Patty and his family. After bringing them up to date on all the events that had occurred since he last corresponded, he concluded with the following reflection:

> 'Time, o time, thou art a fleeting thing.' We had our picture made last week for the senior composite. Add to that a birthday, the changing of the clocks tonight, and the coming of winter, and we find ourselves faced with the rapid passing of our final year in this place.

Seven months we stand from graduation, from the time when we will leave each other to 'go into all the world and preach the gospel.' But thanks to the love that has supported us both from within these walls and without, plus the learning and the sharing that has gone on here, we will be able to survive. And thanks to the gift of God in Christ, we know that we will make it.

> See you soon.
> Love,
> D.

CHAPTER 22

*L*et the words of my mouth, and the medita-
tion of my heart, be acceptable in thy sight,
O Lord, my strength, and my redeemer.
Amen. (Psalm 19:14)

INTRODUCTION

'And he saw and believed.' So goes St. John's
description of the disciple who followed Peter into
the empty tomb on Easter morning.

He saw and believed. These are memorable words
on a most memorable day—the day on which we
commemorate the resurrection of our Lord—the day
when we commemorate the liberation of man from
the finality of death. I ask you to look with me for a
few moments this morning at these words of St. John,
which should always reflect our own response to the
glorious action of God in raising Christ from the dead.

He saw and believed. I choose to look at those
words today in three ways. First, seeing as a prerequisite for believing—the situation. Second, seeing
as a hindrance to believing—the complication. And
third, seeing as a result of believing—the resolution.

FIRST POINT

I like to think that, at least part of the time, I have
what some people would call a logical mind. Therefore,

to me, the most logical way to proceed in this sermon is with seeing as a prerequisite for believing. I find it quite easy to believe in something that I can see. For instance, I believe there are eight people listening to this sermon, because I can see eight people listening to this sermon. The disciple believed the tomb was empty because he could see that the tomb was empty.

But we don't always have to limit our belief to what we can see with our eyes. On a deeper level, we can also see with our emotions, our feelings, and our minds.

When I look at the past two and a half years of seminary, I see more than class notes and more than passing conversations with faculty members and fellow students. I believe that something much more important has gone on than merely what I have been able to see with my eyes.

I believe that learning and new insights into life have also taken place along with class notes. I believe that in addition to conversations with those around me, personal relationships have developed, as well as a better understanding of myself and others.

I believe that disciple understood there was much more going on in an empty tomb than the fact that there was a body missing.

So, not only can we believe in something if we see it with our eyes, but we can also believe in something if we see it with our minds, our feelings, or our emotions.

TRANSITION

But so what? Come on now, preacher. You haven't said very much about yourself, or life, or Easter, if you deal with it in so simplistic a manner. Life is just not so simple. Life is much more complicated. Life demands a more thoughtful look at what it means to see and believe.

SECOND POINT

Allow me, then, to offer another point to consider. Seeing can be a hindrance to believing.

Why? Because, at least for me, believing means trusting in something, putting my faith in something, fulfilling myself in something—something that lasts. How can I believe in something that ends, that has no permanence? And from a human standpoint, all that I see in life will end.

So what that there are eight people listening to my sermon? My sermon will be over in a few minutes. So what that personal relationships here mean so much to me? They will end in seven months. So what that I have gained learning and insights about life in our classes? Life will end one day, just like it did for my father and just as it will for me.

'An empty tomb, so what?' the disciple might have thought. The life of his master was still over, wasn't it?

So, are we left in life without a purpose? From a human point of view, yes. From that point of view, mankind has nothing that lasts in which to believe, nothing of any permanence in which to trust. From that perspective, seeing can be a hindrance to believing.

TRANSITION

So what does an empty tomb on Easter morning say about all of this? And if you accept my argument that seeing can be a hindrance to believing, then what relevance do St. John's words have when he says the disciple 'saw and believed'?

THIRD POINT

That empty tomb gives us something to believe in. When we have nothing in which to believe from a life that ends in death, we do have something to trust in through a life that does not end in death.

When the futility and finality of life offer us nothing in which to have faith, the resurrection of Christ from the grave offers us a fulfillment of life not possible by the hands of man alone.

For me, then, seeing becomes a result of believing. For by believing in Christ, I can see a meaning for my life not otherwise possible. By putting my trust and faith in Christ, who conquered death, my own life becomes fulfilled in Him since I am no longer faced with a hopeless existence over which I have no control.

When that disciple left the empty tomb on Easter morning, he left believing something much more important had taken place than the mere disappearance of a body. Because of the resurrection of his Lord, he was able to see in his own life a purpose—a meaning that encompassed his life fully. His life, then, with all of the people, places, and things that made it what it was, became not something ended by death, but something new and everlasting.

CONCLUSION

Seven months from now, new ministers of the Episcopal Church will go forth from this place 'into all the world to preach the gospel' of Jesus Christ. We will leave behind the classes, the meaningful relationships, and all that has been a part of our life together on this most holy hill. But I pray we never forget that all of those things, as fondly as we may remember them, will ultimately end in death.

In addition, I want us to make sure we remember when we leave here, not to leave behind an empty tomb. I want us to remember to incorporate that empty tomb into our lives and into our ministries, by making sure we incorporate the risen Lord into all we say and do.

I pray we will always believe in a Lord and Savior who has conquered death and who, by His love for us, will forever enable us to see that life is not finalized by death but fulfilled forever in God.

BENEDICTION

A disciple 'saw and believed.' I pray that because we believe, others might see. Amen.

David presented that sermon in academically accepted form to his homiletics class on Thursday, November 5th. It had been a difficult one for him to write, partly because he'd had a hard time composing a piece based on an Easter theme when it was still autumn and partly because he never quite felt sure he had adequately organized his thoughts to say what he really wanted to say. But the task had been to prepare a homily based on the liturgical calendar, and the Tennessean had drawn the feast day of the Resurrection as his assignment.

David had begun working on his sermon the previous Sunday afternoon, and from the outset he'd had a hard time concentrating on the subject matter. That was mainly because Sunday morning field work had focused on the occasion of Hedley's twenty-fifth anniversary as rector of St. George's.

Molle's preaching, as well as a grand reception, high-
lighted the All Saints Day celebration on the first of
November. The congregation gave Father Williams a new
desk, a check for $1,000, and cards of admiration and appre-
ciation from members of his congregation.

The Sunday school classes wrote him expressions of
their affection, and David presented him with a copy of *The
Parables of Peanuts*. Hedley was later to acknowledge that
his senior staff seminarian's inscription, offering thanksgiving to God for their relationship, meant as much to him
as did the book itself.

The remainder of the term passed quickly. On Friday,
November 6th, the Episcureans went out for their monthly
dinner and movie. They chose Blue Hawaii for the restaurant
and the re-release of *It's a Mad, Mad, Mad, Mad World* as
the film.

David had fond memories of that motion picture, for it
was the second show he had seen with Patty, following *How
the West Was Won*. Speaking of that latter title, after over
two months since ordering it, he still hadn't received his
print or heard anything from Auric Enterprises. It was time
to write a letter. He did.

The following Tuesday, David wrote a paper summarizing
his summer experience at Fort Hamilton so that it might be
entered on his seminary transcript as special training. Then
on Friday, the Tennesseans got together for dinner. That
was the last social event of the quarter because finals were
to begin the next week.

For David, that was to consist of one paper due for systematic theology and one examination in Greek. Other than those two requirements, there was only a short paper to write for Christian education. His final grade for homiletics had already been recorded with the sermon he preached back on the 5th of November.

Speaking of grades, the three Wilmerite seniors all did fine. David did fall a little short of an overall "B" average, dropping to a "C" in his language course, but otherwise everything went well. And of course, once again, field education was marked as satisfactory.

David departed for Roanoke and Thanksgiving on Friday, November 20th. More than anything else, his thoughts were with his grandfather who was having cataract surgery that very day. Fortunately, both the trip and the operation turned out well.

Getting into Chattanooga on Saturday night to spend only five full days at home left little time to catch up. But at least David could visit and break bread with his family, as well as be with his beloved Patty, especially enjoying dinner together with Robert and Donna Sessum, before David exited town once again.

Accompanying David back up the road to Virginia was the portable color television set that had belonged to his father. The cross-country traveler felt that vestige of his dad's estate was just the thing to share with his friends for their few remaining months together.

Unfortunately, he knew the gesture would not bring back into their community Ed Mullins, with whom they had enjoyed colorized broadcasting in the past and about his departure from Wilmer Hall, they were still at a loss for a reason. Whenever they had encountered him on campus, their interchanges were cordial but no longer close.

Back at the hill, reunions were joyous even though it had only been a little over a week since their separation. On Sunday, November 29th, David resumed his field work at St. George's. He continued to find the chapel services with the children to be a delight and the confirmation classes with the seventh graders to be a challenge while also trying to fit in the directives to preach, teach, reach, and visit in the home of each member of his group.

Monday came, and so did the beginning of the second quarter. Classes in the offing consisted of another course in systematic theology, a study of New Testament theology, a study of Christian rites and sacraments, and, last but not least, a course in pastoral counseling.

In the 1960s and '70s when a person began preparation for the ministry and entered seminary for the initial quarter of the first year, the majority of classes offered were required. But as one progressed through the curriculum, more and more electives became available. By the time the last year arrived, each student could pretty much create his own course of study.

But all of the seniors seemed interested in taking the same course that term—the first one taught by the new chaplain whom they had all come to love and admire. So on that Monday morning, as the majority of the future graduates filed into Sid Sanders' room and took their seats, he began by saying:

"I know why you guys are here. You guys are here because next year at this time, you're gonna be out in your parishes actually counseling people. And you want to know all of the answers."

Laughter rippled throughout the classroom. Sid continued:

"Well, I'm going to surprise you. I'm gonna give you the answer to fifty-one percent of all the questions from all the counseling sessions you're ever going to have—in one word."

Once again, you could have heard the proverbial pin drop.

"Listen," the chaplain continued. "Fifty-one percent of your people will not be interested as much in answers, as they will be in having someone with whom they can share the questions."

With that introduction, Sid began to outline the components of the course that he planned to cover over the next few weeks. There were a variety of pastoral counseling situations to be dealt with, and each member of the class was to be assigned a seminar to develop. John and David signed up as a team for "Informal and Short Term Counseling Sessions."

Thus, academic life started over. Even though Christmas vacation was only three school weeks away and students continued to find it difficult to hit the books hard, everybody at least made a valiant effort.

Bob, Duck, and John gathered at The Village Inn that Monday night to celebrate another beginning and plan their next meeting of the Episcureans. On Friday, December 4th, they gathered with Jim for dinner at Port of Georgetown then went to see *Little Fauss and Big Halsy* at the Trans Lux Theater.

The next ten days offered nothing unusual; there was only the regimen of scholastic pursuit. But on Tuesday, the 15th, the hall telephone rang. Once more, the ring did not bring a welcome message. That time, the bad news came for the man from Missouri.

The call was to notify John that his grandmother had died. The event carried not quite the depth of emotion as it had with the death of David's father, but even so, John was quite close to her. So once again, a classmate took an unscheduled trip to the airport to bury a loved one.

After seeing his friend off, the man from Tennessee returned to his dorm room to write his tenth seasonal Ember Day letter to the Right Reverend John Vander Horst. After spending some time bringing the bishop up to date on the last few months, the senior wrote the following words of reflection:

> In many ways it does not seem that a joyful time like Christmas is almost upon us. I think of my father who has died, my grandfather who has just undergone surgery, Carl's father who has died, and a close friend who has just lost his grandmother. It is unfortunate that we are not always able to appropriate the happiness of the season. But in times of sorrow, it is comforting to realize and accept the real meaning and glory of the time.

The following Friday after mailing his letter to the prelate and wishing his comrades a holy and happy Christmastide, David steered his VW southwest toward Chattanooga once again with another planned overnight stop at the Roanoke Travel Lodge. Though of course he looked forward to seeing Patty and family members so soon after his last visit—and thankfully for a longer time than he'd had in November— still one thing was bothering him. There was no word yet at all from Auric Enterprises about his print of *How the West Was Won*.

CHAPTER 23

The year 1971 had finally arrived—the year that would mark the end of the seminary experience for Bob, David, and John. It would be a time not only of endings but also of new beginnings, as the three of them prepared to go into the world and preach the gospel of Jesus Christ. But fortunately they still had a few months together before they graduated.

The night of New Year's Day found David settling in at his motel of choice in what had become a most familiar Virginia city on I-81. After sleeping well and driving into Alexandria safely the next afternoon, he was happy to reunite with his friends and share news from the past two weeks. Bob had a wonderful visit with his mother. John had weathered the family funeral and aftermath as well as possible. And the Tennessean finally had some information about his latest film purchase.

In going through some paper work over the holidays, David had discovered one of the old available movie lists from Auric Enterprises. On that sheet of paper was a telephone number that had been marked out, but the new film collector could still make out the digits and decided to give them a try.

He was successful in reaching a man by the name of Wade Williams, who informed him that the first print of

How the West Was Won had been lost during shipment. It had taken a while to locate a new print, and that one should arrive without further delay. Hearing that, David let go a long sigh of relief.

On Sunday, January 3rd, field work resumed. Bob and John were happy to be back at St. Andrew's and St. Francis respectively, while the early Epiphany celebration of the Feast of Lights gave David a wonderful opportunity to continue his ongoing relationship with the people at St. George's.

The next day, academic life commenced for the new year, and everyone quickly got back into the scholastic swing of things. Several other components of noteworthy mention complemented the work week that ensued.

First, David received a letter from the Diocese of Tennessee informing him of an ongoing tradition. Diocesan churchwomen would be giving a present to each graduating seminarian upon the occasion of his being ordained to the diaconate. The gift would consist of an alb, an amice, and a girdle—liturgical vestments used in the celebration of the Holy Eucharist. But as soon as possible, measurements would be needed, as well as any information about other ways in which the ladies might be helpful in the future.

The note could not have been nicer, but for David it raised all kinds of questions in his mind about how qualified he was going to be when he left VTS to move into parish life as a deacon, then priest. Those questions, ones also shared by both Bob and John about their own preparation, were to form the basis of most of the serious discussions the three friends would have during the weeks and months ahead.

By the middle of the week, *How the West Was Won* had finally arrived. David hoisted two boxes from the seminary post office back to his room and counted out another nine reels of 35mm film for which he would need containers. With those nine reels, plus the twelve for *Gone With the Wind* and nine more for *The High and the Mighty*, his collecting ambitions would have to be suspended until after graduation since there simply was no more room left in his closet.

The celluloid collector then went downstairs to the phone booth to call the Wilmo Corporation in Georgetown to place his latest order for shipping cans. As he waited to speak with the proprietor, he was struck by the interesting coincidence of how much the letter "W" was playing in the growth of his new hobby. Wade Williams had sold the product. The supply store was called "Wilmo" and was supervised by a man named Willis Warren.

On Thursday, the 7th, David presented a seminar for his course on Christian rites and sacraments. His topic was "Infant Versus Believer's Baptism," and it proved to be one of the most interesting subjects he dealt with in his entire graduate school life.

The initial focus was on the very nature of sin—its effect on God's people and whether or not man had any real control over the condition. It was an all too appropriate but unfortunate segue to a letter released to the seminary community that very afternoon, announcing the resignation of a member of the faculty.

The reason was understood to be adultery, and it brought home the fact to everyone on the hill that no one—certainly not clergy—was excluded from the inclination toward sin, imperfection, weakness of the flesh, or whatever else anyone wanted to call it.

The incident in its own way emphasized both the truth and the good news of the gospel. Salvation through Christ, as explained in the New Testament, was not dependent on following the letter of Old Testament law or by the number of good works one might have accomplished. Salvation was based solely on God's grace and mankind's response in faith. That did not excuse, however, either sinful behavior or a person's accountability for acts committed. Jesus would have made the distinction this way: the church was called to hate the sin, but love the sinner.

Obviously, given those recent events, the Episcureans had much to talk about at their monthly gathering on the following evening. Discussion took place during dinner at Orleans House before the four headed over to the MacArthur Theater for another movie.

The film selection was *Song of Norway*, and Bob did not care for it at all. He thought it was so bad, in fact, that when the last scene of the picture ended (but before the end credits rolled), the Texan declared: "Thank God it's over."

In that moment of quiet darkness in the theater before the house lights came up, people for several rows around couldn't help but laugh as they stood up to leave. John and Duck were chuckling as well, and they cheerfully signed to Jim what had happened so he could join in the merriment.

Monday, January 11th, ushered in the annual parish meeting at St. George's. As David prepared to drive to the church that evening, he offered up a silent prayer for John, who was sequestered in his room over several nights taking canonical examinations. What other seniors didn't have to worry about until after graduation, the Diocese of West Missouri required of its students in course. All who knew the seminary football official, however, only hoped that when their time came to take their exams, they would do as well.

The following Monday, details were released about the annual gift to be presented by the seniors to their alma mater.

John and David had both served on a committee that arrived at a consensus to establish a revolving loan fund, thereby making money available to students in need, asking only that the amount be paid back when or if convenient. Each member of the class was subsequently asked to make an initial contribution of $100. David was happy because the gift would complement well the work of the Student Aid Society.

That same day, David found himself beginning his assignment as "senior of the week" in chapel. Responsibilities entailed being available for the office of Morning Prayer on Monday, Wednesday, and Thursday, as well as for celebrations of the Eucharist, both at the new petition-approved service on Tuesday morning, and the regular Thursday evening seminary community gathering.

Duties included reading lessons at Morning Prayer and then either reading the epistle for the day or administering the chalice at Holy Communion. Middlers read the prayer for the whole state of Christ's Church and acted as acolytes. Juniors read the Old Testament lesson and took up the offering. Of course, there were also potential duties assigned to any and all of the above as sacristans.

Later that same week as David headed for a vestry meeting at St. George's, his car skidded on a frozen stretch of the highway and slid off the road into an embankment. He was not hurt, but Sam, the Volkswagen, did suffer—to the tune of $500 for the repair of a bent axle.

If that sort of thing had to happen, however, the timing could not have been better. David was able to put his automobile in the shop for the few days he would be out of town preaching a Theological Education Sunday sermon at his home parish near Chattanooga. The message he delivered was to be the same one he would give the following Sunday at his field work site. His words to both congregations were a fairly good summary of where he considered himself to be at that point in the learning process.

Preaching that sermon in his home parish was obviously a very special occasion. In essence, it was a culmination of all that had gone on before in Tennessee. Returning to the hill after such a brief trip home was hard for David, but fortunately, Patty was planning to fly in just a few days later.

David returned to Virginia to discover that in his absence, the board of trustees had decided to convert his anticipated Bachelor of Divinity degree to a Master in Divinity degree. For a long time, the title had been designated bachelor level because there were no specific undergraduate requirements for entering the seminary.

But at one particular meeting of the governing body, someone made the point that no undergraduate requirements for any degree really began until one's third year in college. If you were to add to that a year of postgraduate study for a master's, you would wind up with a three year program. The three years of seminary, therefore, should qualify for a master's degree.

The opinion swayed the board, and the class members of 1971 would become the first to be awarded master's degrees upon the occasion of seminary graduation. That news, the dean himself told David when he called on Cecil in order to bring him greetings from David's mother and grandfather.

Thus, entering the academic work week of January 25th, David found himself riding on an emotional high. Classes were going well, and he was beginning to feel more and more confident in seeing himself as a minister of the Episcopal Church. For his field work evaluation, the future graduate attempted to summarize his observations to date:

In my first year of seminary, I was a believer in books as preparation for the ministry. My second year, I discovered through field work that the ministry was all about people. Now in my third and final year, as relationships deepen, I see more and more the need for incorporation of books into what we do, in order to relate as well as possible to those in need. One has to accept people where they are, understand them in that light, then help them with the knowledge one has acquired—not impose preconceived ideas on them.

My experience at St. George's has offered me an opportunity to work with all age levels—children, youth, and adults. Both the formal and the informal aspects of services and coffee hours, as well as the teaching and business facets of classes and vestry meetings, have enabled me to observe people on different levels.

My most valuable experience so far probably has been leading a confirmation class, because when I discovered that the course outline I had planned wasn't going to work, I had to change it. So, I must constantly be able to modify my approach to fit the needs of a changing church and a changing world. Relating the real message of Christianity is not always as easy as it might seem.

David felt good about his review session with Hedley that day, and as he drove back to campus in his newly repaired vehicle, he began to look forward to the arrival of a certain young lady that coming Friday.

Eastern Airlines whisked Patty in from Tennessee by way of Atlanta on January 29th. David picked her up, and they headed to the home of Roy and Gail, who had extended an invitation for weekend lodging. After visiting with the Greens a while, they called it a night.

On Saturday, the reunited couple had breakfast at the International House of Pancakes and that afternoon, watched *How the West Was Won* in room #207 of the dorm. By that time the latest order of shipping cans had arrived, so David was able to secure his latest nine reels of film in protective cases after viewing. That night, they went over to Carl and Nelia Cunningham's for dinner.

The first day of the week came all too quickly; it was time to part company once again. But the special woman in the life of the preacher in the pulpit at St. George's that Sunday was not willing to leave town without being present, as she had been the week before, to hear the words of his TEO sermon.

'Let the words of my mouth, and the meditation of my heart, be acceptable in thy sight, O Lord, my strength, and my redeemer.' Amen.

This day is devoted to the seminarian. Theological Education Sunday is a time for the ministerial student to bring the congregation, in some way, to a current understanding of what's going on in the world of the divinity school. The chosen representative, which I have the honor of being this morning, can usually approach that theme in one of three ways.

He can tackle it from quite an elementary point of view and merely recite his daily schedule. He can approach it from a campaign point of view, since seminaries are always in need of money, as are most centers of learning. Or he can file those first two by title, as I have chosen, and attempt to do what he feels called to do—preach the gospel.

Many of us students travel on this particular Sunday to preach in different areas of the country either far away or close to home. We carry with us a packet of information prepared by our development office, which gives us assorted facts, figures, and information about VTS. And also listed are a series of biblical passages from which one might prepare a sermon.

My text this morning comes from the lessons appointed for December 27th, the feast day of St. John, apostle and evangelist. From the Gospel of John I quote a request made by Jesus to Peter, a statement that applies to us today—both you and me—a command that suggests not only the reason that I am preparing for the ministry, but also a challenge that faces all of us every day of our lives. I quote two words: 'Follow me.'

Not often have I seen a statement so concise and to the point yet so all encompassing and important. But just what does it mean to 'Follow me'? I would like to approach that question from three different angles: Who is it that we follow? How do we follow Him? And why do we follow Him?

First, who is it that we follow? Perhaps we can best answer that question by looking at the season of Christmas, which has just passed, and its real meaning. Hopefully, when we get through all the cards, shopping, and busyness of the season, we remember that we are really celebrating the birth of Jesus Christ. We are celebrating the identification of God with man. We are celebrating the coming of God in human form or, as one small child once put it, 'God with skin on.'

Many times in our lives, I feel that we think of God only as a concept, topic, theme, or theory, and it is often quite difficult to put that sort of thing into any kind of practical use. But with the coming of God in Christ, man at last has a concrete example that he can both understand and follow, a perfect example of the God whom he worships within the confines of his own humanity and world, a perfect example of perfect love.

How then do we respond to that love of God? How then do we react to that example? How then do we follow Him? The answer may seem somewhat obvious as far as I'm concerned. I am a man who has chosen the ministry as his vocation. I am a man who has chosen to follow Christ for his occupation and livelihood. But my professional choice is only a reflection and indication of the same question that I share with each and every person in this church. And that question is: How do I serve God with my life? How do I follow Him in my day-to-day existence? How do I preach the gospel?

Preach the gospel. It has always interested me that the word is 'preach,' not 'teach.' 'Teach' speaks to me of words. 'Preach' speaks to me of example.

Several months ago, I was getting my children's chapel service off the ground. Some of the kids were new; some were a little frightened at the newness of it all. And one little boy, who found himself to be too short of stature to reach the candle he was trying to light, began to cry. I tried everything in my power to get him to stop, but nothing seemed to work. Finally empty of words, I simply smiled at him. I had nothing left to give except some small expression that showed that I cared. But that turned out to be the most meaningful thing I could have done. The child stopped crying and smiled back at me.

'Out of the mouths of babes,' as the saying goes. 'If I speak in the tongues of men and of angels, but have not love,' St. Paul says, 'I am a noisy gong or a clanging cymbal.' It took a child to show that to me. How then do we respond to the love of God? We respond with love itself.

Last spring my father died. Up until then, I had always wondered just what words I might use to comfort someone at the death of a loved one. But at that time in my own life, I discovered it was not important what was said or even done. All that really mattered to me was that there were people surrounding me. All that really mattered was that there were people with me who cared. All that was important was the love I felt.

So why is it that when I look around at our world today, I find people facing identity crises, pessimistic about their futures, unsure of what they believe in, questioning whether or not they have the ability to help or love, or be helped or loved by anyone? Why is it that so many of us are frustrated by life?

Certainly we cannot find a simple answer for all of those questions. But is it not possible that part of the explanation lies in the fact that we have lost what we believe in? Are we trying to do it all by ourselves? Are we trying to get ourselves all figured out, the problems of the world solved, and the answers to all of the questions in our minds given before we are at ease? Is it possible then that, even though we say we believe in Jesus Christ, think we understand who He is, and know how we are supposed to follow Him, we may have forgotten the real reason as to why?

Why then do we follow Him? We follow Him because He is our Lord and our Savior. Christmas is not a complete story. It has to be fulfilled in Easter. The earthly life and way of love that Jesus led are not complete until the death and resurrection of Christ takes place. Consequently, the earthly life of man is not complete until it is seen in the light of the gift, the glory, and the joy of Jesus Christ. Not only did God live like us, He died for us—for our failures, for our sins, and for our salvation. That is the real gospel. That is the real good news.

And that is quite a joyful realization. I can think back now to that chapel service and know that my relationship with God does not depend on whether I stopped that child from crying. I can be thankful that my ultimate salvation is not based on whether I am successful in my chosen profession. And I can go to my father's grave, knowing that is not all there is, knowing I will see him again.

I wish that I could stand here and give you the answers to all of the questions, problems, and fears that we will have in our lives. And we do have them, don't we? I guess one of the hardest things we ever have to admit to ourselves is that we are not perfect, that we will not and cannot save the world by ourselves. But, thank God, it is not all up to us. What a blessing, what a relief it is to know the gift of God, to know that God knows we are not perfect, and to know that God takes the ultimate burden of life upon Himself.

And in that sense we have a freedom not otherwise possible. Now we can go together 'into all the world and preach the gospel,' spread the good news, knowing whom we follow (Jesus Christ), knowing how we follow (with our lives and with our love), and knowing why we follow (because He is our Savior, and our Lord). Amen.

CHAPTER 24

Roy had not been back in Wilmer Hall to visit his friends since he married Gail, and although the trip on Wednesday, February 3rd, was more for business than for pleasure, it was a happy reunion. The Floridian had signed on with CM Almy Company as a seminary field representative for their vestment line and was in the dorm to take orders. Bob, David, and John had their lists prepared, and they all chose practically the same things, as they began to think in terms of new clothing for the future. Seven shirts, three collars, three pairs of collar buttons, one rabat, one cincture, three t-shirts, one tippet, two VTS seals, one surplice, and one hood came to a total of $119.10 apiece.

Dr. Reid had kicked off the month as minister of the week—the academic week, at least, which concluded on Friday with the latest outing of the Episcureans. The gang went to El Tio Pepe in Georgetown for a delectable Spanish/ Mexican meal and then to see the re-release of *Marooned*, playing once again at the Uptown Theater where Patty and David had seen it one year earlier.

The next day, John and David got their hands on a huge screen upon which to present *How the West Was Won* in as close to its original Cinerama format as possible. The patented wide-screen process required a deeply arched viewing surface. They did not have total success in curving the screen correctly, but it was successful enough to once again guarantee an evening of fun and entertainment for the seminary community.

When February 9th arrived, a Tuesday to be exact, the country watched as Apollo 14 successfully splashed down into the Pacific after nine days in space, including thirty-three hours on the moon. That return was the same day that another humorous occurrence took place in Wilmer Hall, once again involving Dave Upton (the dorm member who had locked out the interminable shower-taker, Geoff Price). It seems Upton had a penchant for really hot jalapeños. His mouth must have been lined with asbestos, because he could bite through those things without blinking an eye.

Staying in the dorm at the time was the Reverend John Ling, visiting the seminary from Taiwan for a study program in Anglican theology. John was a likeable guy who joined in with the other Wilmerites for hall prayers and various outings.

That Tuesday evening, several members of the dorm were gathered in Upton's room while he consumed his favorite delicacy when in came Father Ling. Dave offered everyone one of his peppers, but of course no one present was reckless enough to take him up on it, with one exception.

For Father Ling, the opportunity to experience a new American treat was too much of a temptation to refuse. In hindsight, he shouldn't have tried it without a glass of water—or a fire extinguisher—in hand.

Father John took a big bite out of his sample just as Dave had. But while Upton sat there chewing, the Taiwan visitor's eyes began to water and his nostrils to burn. He even suspected steam was seeping out of his ears.

The hall residents stood aside so their new friend could dash out of the room to drink the hall water fountain dry. Needless to say, the Reverend John Ling never tried one of those peppers again.

On a much more serious note, the following day VTS issued a statement concerning the subject of homosexuality. It did not come as a great surprise to anyone. The Episcopal Church had been dealing with the issue for years. But the fact that there was a position paper on it caused a great deal of discussion, including a late night conversation for Bob, David, and John.

In essence, the printed policy acknowledged that there continued to be a lot of discussion about the nature of human sexuality—about whom people are attracted to, why they are attracted to them, and whether or not such relationships are right or wrong. But as far as the institutional church was concerned, the only accepted practice of sexual expression was that between husband and wife within the sanctified bond of Holy Matrimony.

That statement was sufficient as far as some members of the community were concerned but inadequate for others. As minister of the week, Chaplain Sid Sanders preached an excellent sermon at the Thursday community service, which reminded everybody what was really important about the current issue: as imperfect human beings, no one can sit in judgment of another because everyone falls short of the glory of God.

The chaplain reminded members of the congregation about the scene at the Last Supper between Jesus and His disciples. When Christ told them that one of those gathered around the table would betray Him, not one of the future apostles professed an inability to do such a thing. Knowing his own potential weakness, each one of them was forced to ask the question: "Is it I, Lord?" Those present for the message that evening left the chapel filled with new food for thought.

Then, all of a sudden it seemed, the end of another quarter arrived. John and David had already found themselves busy planning their next trip to the Big Apple in the spring, not yet willing to face the fact that it would be their last. But that point was driven home soon enough, because on Friday night, the 12th, the Dean and Mrs. Woods hosted an early farewell party for the senior class.

Lanky Jim Alby accompanied David on that cold winter's night to walk to the party, where they joined their fellow classmates for a fine meal and a fun night. The occasion offered one more example of how close faculty and students were becoming, thanks to those kinds of social engagements. The following Sunday was St. Valentine's Day, and the Tennessean did indeed love the moments he spent talking by phone with his girl.

Everyone was busy the last two weeks of the term, preparing final classroom presentations, working on course assignments, and finishing up required papers. David had one of his better quarters, making a "B" in three of his subjects, plus an "A" from Chaplain Sid in pastoral counseling. Once again, field education was marked as satisfactory.

David also took time before he left on break to write his Ember Day letter a little early. That way, not only did he keep from having to worry about doing it while on vacation but also it allowed him a chance to find out if the rumor was true—that his bishop had suffered a heart attack. Jack Vander Horst was quick to reply that it was only chest discomfort and high blood pressure. But because of his doctor's counsel, he was not going to be able to make his annual visit, which was a disappointment for all concerned.

Also included in the response was some initial information about parish placement following graduation. Though no specific site had yet been determined, it was nice to know that the wheels were in motion. David would need at least three years of experience with a congregation before he could go on active duty as a military chaplain.

Speaking of the chaplaincy, when David departed for Roanoke on Friday, February 26th, he left the hill having completed an article for publication in the latest edition of *Ambo* regarding that very subject. It seemed there had been some questions on campus, raised specifically by the recent consecration of a new bishop for the armed forces, about whether or not there really was a need to have military ministers. The man from Tennessee had felt that he needed to address that issue in an *Ambo* column.

Chaplain?

The title that I have given this article seems to me to be most appropriate, for I find the role of the military chaplain to be in serious question today. When I was in college and enrolled in the Reserve Officers Training Corps, it seemed only logical to me, since I was going into the ministry, to accept a commission and fulfill my service time in the chaplains' branch. There was no great wrenching of conscience at the time, only what I considered to be taking an obvious step.

Five years later, however, with the progression

of the war in Viet Nam, the present attitude of the country toward the military, and more recently the consecration of a new bishop for the armed forces, I find myself writing at a time when certain questions need to be asked and answered, certain issues resolved, and certain conclusions drawn. Of course, any statement I make will be a personal one, but I feel obligated to make it.

Though on the ministerial side of things, I have no more valid a voice than anyone else at this institution, I do offer on the military side several reasons as to why my opinion should be considered: hours of conversations with chaplains as well as other short term and career soldiers both in and out of the service; interviews with those in authority about the military chaplaincy; talks with both the current and future bishop for the armed forces, Arnold Lewis and Clarence Hobgood. Also, last summer I attended the nine-week orientation course at the United States Army Chaplain School, Fort Hamilton, Brooklyn, New York.

To describe the program, let me say that it was mostly classroom work, based on an 8:00 to 5:00 day. Those in attendance covered a wide range: from seminarians like myself who had completed either one or two years of theological education to parish priests with no military experience, from military men coming into the chaplaincy from other branches to experienced chaplains themselves, from those on or coming onto active duty to those in reserve units.

In light of the diverse backgrounds, not to mention the variety of denominations represented, the academic program was structured on a twofold plan to delineate the role of the military and the role of chaplain.

The military courses were aimed basically at those who had not benefited from previous army experience and who knew little to nothing about that organization. Therefore lectures were in order on army organization, military courtesy, and missions of the various branches.

The courses oriented toward the role of a chaplain, however, were more interesting for all concerned. Four components of the curriculum stand out in my mind:

First, Character Guidance, a program for the young serviceman, usually led by a chaplain but not necessarily from a religious perspective. Classes focus on acquainting the soldier with the basic moral heritage of our country.

Second, The Chaplain and his Environment, a course dealing with some of the more common problems in the system that a chaplain has to face. Included are subjects like racism, drugs, as well as the very military structure itself.

Third, Psychology and Counseling, which is much the same training as the civilian minister undertakes but just more military oriented. Major issues might include young men and women away from home for the first time or men in the crisis of battle.

And fourth, Pastoral Relationships and Responsibilities, emphasizing the role of the chaplain as a minister both for and to the soldier. The chaplain is a man there for the military person to talk to, a man who offers some kind of identification with the world that the soldier used to know, and, most importantly, a man of God, a man of love, and a friend.

There is, however, a deeper concern about the military chaplaincy that needs to be addressed here. In last October's issue of *The Episcopalian*, an article was entitled 'Should Chaplains Be Military Men?' The piece is a criticism not of the people who are called to that particular ministry but of the system that surrounds it. The central question raised is whether or not a chaplain has any real ability to minister to his people.

Can he really function effectively if he is part of an institution structured in ways that could limit his freedom as a minister and, at the same time, make him part of an environment that embraces the moral ambiguity of war? This is a valid question—one that many of us had as we entered the program. But I believe we all came out with both a satisfactory and workable answer.

The emphasis throughout the curriculum was on the chaplain first of all as a minister and lastly as an officer. A chaplain should be looked upon as a civilian in uniform. One who does not have to sacrifice his identity for the sake of a system.

Now I'm not denying the possibility that does indeed exist of some people going into the chaplaincy either because they can't make it in parish ministry, need the authority of a system to back them up, or are just plain gung-ho military. But any opinion of them inside the service is just as low as is found outside.

It certainly is not that type of man who is causing the military establishment to respect more and more

the chaplain and his role. Because of the unsettling
times in which we live—the ambiguities, doubts,
and questions that face us all—and the highly edu-
cated people coming into military service, the army
chaplain is finding himself in a position of greater
responsibility than ever before.

And it is because the chaplain is being heeded,
understood, and listened to more and more that all
parties desire the military minister to be an officer, to
be part of the system. How else can he really be available, how else can he understand what an individual
is going through, and how else can he do anything
about it?

I had a member of my field work parish ask me
this past fall how I could rationalize being both
a man of God and part of a system structured for
war. It was only after prayerful thought that I could
respond in a way that allowed us both to come to
a reasonable understanding of just what the chaplain's role is in the service. That same parishioner
later asked me to write a letter of support for his
request for conscientious objection. Several people
here at seminary could not understand how I could
write that sort of letter if I were going into the service myself.

Some clarification is needed here. A chaplain
is not a warmonger—not in the army because he
believes in killing for Christ. He's not a minister who
feels that the army has a perfect system or always a
right way of doing things. (In fact, one of his biggest
jobs is writing letters for conscientious objectors.)
We are talking here about a man of God, a man who
answers a call to a special congregation. He is a man

of God who ministers to others within the military system.

In the course of the program last summer, we spent one week at Fort Dix, a basic training camp in New Jersey. During those few days, the members of my class were assigned as individual chaplains to the basic trainee units. And in talking with those men, I saw for myself how much a military pastor is needed by the soldiers—for ministry, for advice, and for friendship.

I saw and talked with men in service for the first time, some even in their first week, questioning how to serve both God and country, too, and wondering how to solve problems—problems they could discuss with no one else but a chaplain. And I was surprised at the pastoral impact I had because I was an officer, for there were men in that place who were thankful to have officers who did something besides give orders, thankful to have officers with whom they could just talk.

It has been some time since I made that initial decision to become a chaplain, but in that time I have only reaffirmed that decision. What I have written in this article attests to that fact, as it does to the caliber of men I saw last summer. Regardless of the variety of backgrounds and denominations, I found a group of people united in a common bond; bound together to serve both God and His people in a unique way, a sacrificial way, a needed way. I lived with these men, I worshiped with them, and it was a fulfilling pleasure to have done so.

With the problems of the world the way they are in Vietnam and in the Middle East, with turmoil and strife both in our world and in our society, and with everything changing so fast that we hardly know what's going on anymore, the young people of today go into an army unsure not only of what they face, but why. Someone must be there to fight that fight with them. I know that the caliber of man I saw last summer is able to meet that challenge.

So, I ask you in your thoughts and prayers to remember a special type of minister and a special kind of congregation. I ask you to remember the chaplain and the soldier. And I ask you always to pray for the whole state of Christ's Church and the world.

CHAPTER 25

After a restful few days at home, David departed Chattanooga for his final trip to seminary, stopping once again in Roanoke. It was Friday, the 5th of March, Patty's birthday, and he wished more than anything that she could be with him for the journey. Patty was busy with her X-ray training program, however, and even though she was given a nice surprise party by her dorm mates, she also wished that the two of them could be together.

The man from Tennessee had a restful night at the Travel Lodge, naturally having seen a film before turning in. His drive northward through Virginia was an uneventful one, although he did find himself savoring every minute and every mile, since it was to be his last trip east to VTS.

He arrived safely back on campus in time to get settled and take in yet one more movie before picking up John at the airport. Bob had remained on the hill for spring break and was happy to reunite with his friends at The Village Inn that evening. Over pizza, salad, and beer, they shared their individual news from the past week—including the general news they all had heard that their former dorm mate Ted Boswell was not only married but the father of a new baby as well.

After nightly exchange of the seminarian blessing with John, David closed his door for a glass of milk and a couple of cookies before bed. He could not help but notice the calendar on his desk, and as the daily date was torn from its comrades, once more the desire arose in him to savor every remaining moment of time together with friends and brothers in Christ.

Field work resumed on Sunday, and the last academic quarter started on Monday, March 8th. Courses were to be in parish administration, youth ministry, homiletics, and personal religion. That last offering allowed the seniors one last chance to study with their chaplain, Sid Sanders. Topics to be discussed in seminar format would include the nature of prayer, providence, doubt, adoration, confession, thanksgiving, intercession, petition, and the nature of an anthropomorphic God. Each of the class members would keep a personal daily journal to record prayerful aspects of an ongoing relationship with the Lord. Except for Thursday afternoons, all courses were to be offered in the morning hours.

However, the term was delayed in getting started because on that Monday morning, everyone woke up to find that a late winter storm had dumped a good deal of snow and ice. Northern Virginia was immobilized for about seventy-two hours, but the campus looked beautiful, all dressed up in its new white coat. At lunch, Molle said it all reminded him that a good snowball fight had not taken place around there in a long time, and it might be a good way for the senior class to ease some of the tension they could be feeling with graduation just around the corner.

Wilmerites were not slow to pick up the ball. For three days, they fortified themselves on the roof top of the archway connecting their dorm to St. John's. Both faculty and students had great fun as they tried to dislodge the defending forces from their perch. Finally it all came to an end, and only David had managed to escape being soaked by an onslaught of bombarding snowballs.

In honor of his achievement, a special announcement was made at lunch in the refectory on Thursday. John invited the Tennessean up to the podium to receive a much-deserved award, and then to a round of applause, John very carefully pushed one last snowball into David's face.

Things got back to normal after that, just in time for the annual college conference on the ministry, which was scheduled to take place that weekend. The man from Missouri shared in the leadership for the overall event, the official title of which was "Ministry In The Seventies: A Realistic View." David kept the registration desk, Bob administered bedding, and Jim took care of the linens. About forty single men participated, and when it was all over John was very tired but pleased with the success of it.

That same weekend, on Saturday the 13th of March to be exact, David received a letter from Bishop Vander Horst announcing his placement as a deacon-in-training. He was to be assigned to the Reverend James Coleman at St. John's in Johnson City, Tennessee.

"He's a good man, and you should have holy fun," the prelate commented.

The recipient of the letter had mixed feelings: relief that there was something definite in the future on which to focus but regret that his seminary experience was about to end.

Sunday arrived, and it seemed that warmer weather might finally be coming, as the season of spring inched closer. David preached that morning at St. George's, focusing once again as he had done the previous year, on the Academy Award nominations for best picture of the year.

Jim had expressed once an opinion to his cinema-loving friend, that if Jesus were still to be teaching, He would use movies as a medium for conveying His thoughts, just as He used parables in His own time. David had not forgotten that point, especially as he waxed eloquently on the nominees.

He made reference to the fact that all five films were like parables, each one of them trying in its own way to convey some truth or moral lesson in story form. Since each tale described an attempt to seek fulfillment in life, the preacher drove home his message that ultimately a quest of that magnitude could only be made complete by a relationship with Jesus Christ.

Continuing with that same motion picture theme Sunday night, David showed *The High and the Mighty* to members of his youth group. John was there, as always, to assist as co-projectionist.

On Friday, March 19th, (late that month because of vacation and the college conference) the Episcureans were finally able to gather. They ate dinner at The Chaparral, a restaurant on top of the Marriott Hotel at Key Bridge, then saw *Cromwell* at the MacArthur Theater. It was another delightful evening and just about the last one the four of them would share before another onslaught took place, namely the influx of things that needed to be done before graduation.

For David at least, that deluge did not start off too badly. At the beginning of the next week, he found himself the recipient of a check for $100, along with a nice note from the rector and vestry of his home parish, expressing their hope that the money would help with closing things out at the end of the year.

On the following day, however, the mail was not quite as appealing. What arrived was the written examination from the Diocese of Tennessee in general church history and historical theology. Enumerated therein were some eight questions, including one on a special period or topic of interest in the field of church history to be selected by the student.

Each question was to be developed within one hour, the entire test was to be self-administered in as many sittings as needed, and the whole thing was to be returned to the diocesan office by the middle of May. The intent of the written work, of course, was to take some of the pressure off of preparation for canonical examinations following graduation.

The mail of March 25th brought the list of requirements to be met before ordination to the diaconate could be approved. One bit of good news was the elimination of the need to submit copies of sermons.

The title of the special period or topic of church history selected for examination was to be in the hands of the chairman of the diocesan commission on ministry by the end of April. And the standing committee required that the following be on file by May 23rd:

(a) A personal application to become ordained, written in one's own handwriting and stating the date of birth.

(b) A certificate from a priest of the church known to the ecclesiastical authority—the form to be followed according to canon law. (Hedley would do the honors for David.)

(c) A certificate from the rector and vestry of the student's home parish, following the form of canon law.

(d) A certificate from the seminary showing the student's scholastic record in required subjects and a statement expressing judgment as to the qualification of the individual for the ministry of the church.

(e) A favorable medical and psychological report.

Both of those last two tests went fine for David. In fact, he was to remember for a long time his interview with the assigned psychiatrist. The only time the doctor took copious notes was while David reflected on the death of his father and what he had learned from that tragic experience—that his faith was strengthened, not weakened, by it.

Before they knew it, April had arrived—the next to the last month the Wilmerites would spend together. The annual married couples conference on the ministry was held on the first weekend, beginning the evening of Friday, the 2nd. That was the same night the Episcureans dined at Blackbeard's, then viewed *The Night Visitor* at the Dupont Theater.

Holy Week began two days later with services on Palm Sunday. Other than taking a few hours to watch the Academy Awards presentation on Tuesday, the 6th, study time on the weekdays and weeknights that followed was spent not only on class work but also on all that canonical paperwork to be mailed in. David spent a considerable amount of time trying to get everything he had to do organized into a manageable system. About that, John was to comment:

"Duck, you waste time more constructively than anybody I've ever known."

Somehow, by the grace of God, everything seemed to move in perfect order. On Good Friday David experienced not only sadness as he commemorated the first anniversary of the death of his father but also elation at the arrival of his beloved Patty for Easter weekend.

Once again, she stayed with Mil Ritchie in Arlington, and

once again they had a couple of days to enjoy each other's company over brunches and dinners. And, of course, they celebrated their hours together with at least one movie, choosing to see *The Andromeda Strain* at the Apex Theater.

But all too soon, it was time to part. Patty headed back to Chattanooga to prepare for her X-ray registry examination, while David got back to the work before him. He had one scare which concerned him early that next week, however—a rough hospital stay for his mother for the removal of her gall bladder. Fortunately, she came through it relatively well.

On April 13th, the mail brought David back quickly to the reality of the paperwork before him. Future boss Jim Coleman had written, not in his capacity as an employer but in his role as a canonical examining chaplain, asking the senior seminarian to name a synoptic gospel and epistle on which to be tested.

All of that paperwork, of course, had to be completed while the remainder of the academic year was ticking away. Fortunately, the courses in the last quarter were not too challenging.

Everyone still loved Sid Sanders, so the personal religion class was going well, especially the required hours of reflection and meditation, which helped to ease the otherwise hectic schedule of activity. Most of what was being talked about in youth ministry class was being lived out in field work. And homiletics continued to offer opportunities to practice preaching. That left only parish administration with which to take issue.

The formal title of the course was Parish Administration and Canon Law. And though everybody liked Professor Henry Rightor, they were not particularly pleased that he was using so much valuable class time to expound on his own personal views supporting the ordination of women.

That was not to say all of the class members disagreed with his position on the subject. Some did; some didn't. It was just that there were other issues that needed to be addressed, and they weren't getting the attention they deserved. Very little, if anything, was being learned about canon law and parish administration.

The teacher argued that most of what students really needed to know could be either gotten out of their textbook or picked up once they entered into parish ministry. He preferred to use class time to talk about what was considered to be the next great frontier for the Episcopal Church.

Henry, however, was never one to take himself too seriously. And the course actually wound up being a lot of fun, once everyone else figured that out. Interestingly enough, the subject matter, which was supposed to be the focal point of study in the first place, got more emphasis from a letter the instructor handed out than from anything else said or done the entire quarter.

The epistle was addressed to Professor Rightor and came from a parish priest who had taken the course in question while in seminary. With three and a half years of ministry under his belt, the author was writing to make a few suggestions for revision of that particular part of the curriculum.

Composed with tongue in cheek, he offered the following suggestions:

> 1. Each person should be required to obtain a certificate of proficiency in the areas of electric wiring and maintenance. A knowledge of how to service air-conditioning and heating units might also be in order. This is assuming that most seminary graduates already know how to load and light a coal stove.

2. Each graduate who intends to be a parish priest should be required to graduate from an accredited law school. This would be in order to keep up with changing diocesan rules, regulations, canons, etc. It would also help if he knew whether or not he could actually be sued for referring to "sin" in a sermon.

3. There should be offered a course called "How to Read an Insurance Policy" as it applies to church and rectory insurance.

4. Forget the part about dealing with a church treasurer in a pastoral way and substitute a course in bookkeeping for beginners and how to fire your treasurer in a pastoral way when he takes off with the parish funds and the daughter of the chairman of the altar guild.

5. A practicum in roof repair would be of immeasurable value, as would something in basement bailing.

6. Pastoral responsibility to the vestry could be removed and a seminar added that would be concerned with finding people willing to serve on a vestry in the first place.

7. My secretary, who has been reading over my shoulder due to the fact that she neither types nor takes dictation, suggests that there should also be a course offered in the repair and maintenance of mimeograph machines, typewriters, prying open stuck file drawers, and rewiring coffee pots.

The letter was signed "Faithfully, George." Needless to say, the entire class got a real kick out of the comments, especially the last sentence above the signature line: "Actually, aside from the fact that I found P.A. totally lacking in any practical value, I enjoyed it very much."

On Friday, April 16th, the second farewell party for the senior class was held at the deanery. The idea of having two good-bye teas was based on the assumption that not everyone would be available to attend on any one specific date. It also meant that some of the seminarians might have the opportunity to visit twice in the home of the Woods—like Bob, John, and David.

The following night, David dined in the home of Carl and Nelia Cunningham for the last time before graduation. They couldn't help but reminisce about the infamous dinner with the Bishop of Tennessee held there a couple of years earlier. All three of them were to wonder if they would ever have such interesting meals together again.

The next week found David closing out his year as president of the Student Aid Society, and on Thursday he handed over the gavel to his successor. It had been a good twelve months, or actually only a little over eleven, in the presiding chair of an organization that was designed solely for the purpose of helping people in need.

David thought about some of those folks as he packed that evening after the weekly community service. Hard as it was to believe, he and John were on the threshold of their last spring trip to New York. Friday Bob drove them to Union Station, where they caught the one o'clock Metroliner.

Having eaten a bite on the train and arrived in Manhattan right at 4:00, the travelers took a cab back to The Americana. There was plenty of time to enjoy the view from the room, unpack, and relax for a while before getting ready for dinner.

John and David decided to give Mamma Leone's, with the menu printed only in Italian, another try. Even though the diners remembered not to order from every course listed, as they had done before, there was still too much food to finish. Upon departing, the realization dawned on the two friends that, alas, "Mamma" had done them in for two years in a row.

Chuckling over their failure ever to get the best of the restaurant, the seniors headed off for their first play of the trip. *Sleuth*, a mystery, was playing at the Music Box Theater, and that selection offered them a most enjoyable evening, which could only have been complemented by a walk over to Times Square to take in the lights of Broadway before calling it a night.

Saturday greeted the visitors with a room service breakfast before their sightseeing began with a morning excursion to the United Nations Headquarters. The tour was most informative, and the experience of being at that historical site was quite a thrill.

A quick bite back at the hotel allowed them ample time to get ready for the matinée performance of the musical *Hair*, which was playing at the Biltmore Theater. Unfortunately, the most memorable event of the afternoon happened not in the auditorium, but in the men's rest room. As David freshened up before the curtain rose, the man from Missouri bent over to tie his shoe. A loud rip ensued. The center seam of John's new suit had given way—right in the seat of his trousers. Needless to say, he walked very carefully until they returned to The Americana.

Given the time it took to sew up the pants, the two friends decided to dine at their hotel that evening before venturing over to see *Applause*, a musical playing at the Palace Theater, the same place where two years earlier they had seen *George M!* And because it was their last night in New York, the travelers just had to pay one last visit to Times Square before they prepared to lose another precious hour to daylight saving time.

After another room service breakfast on Sunday, John and David took a morning cruise over to Staten Island and back, giving them a chance to see things in the light of day, as opposed to their night visit there in 1969. And after checking out of the hotel, they still had time to visit the Empire State Building once more, to say "so long" to the city they had come to love visiting each spring.

Retrieving their bags from the hotel, the seniors took another cab to Penn Station for an afternoon departure on the Metroliner back to Washington. As they enjoyed a pleasant meal on the train, they reflected not only on the past three days, but reminisced about their earlier trips to New York as well. The companions knew they would have fond memories for years to come. Bob and Flo were waiting to greet them at Union Station and to take them back home to the hill.

CHAPTER 26

The month of May proved to be a time of commencement in more ways than one. On Saturday, the 1st, Amtrak began operation of intercity rail service across the country. Had David and John planned their trip northward for that weekend, they would have experienced a new management system. But the two comrades were occupied on that Saturday night with showing *How the West Was Won* to Bob's youth group at St. Andrew's in Arlington. That was to be the last time they worked together as movie projectionists.

At the beginning of the next week, the Tennessean paid a visit to Willis Warren at the Wilmo Corporation in Georgetown. There he was able to purchase the 35mm portable projector he had been renting, as well as arrange for not only that item but also all of his film prints as well to be crated and shipped to him once he got settled in Johnson City. Having thanked the businessman for the relationship they had shared, the collector returned to Wilmer Hall, grateful that his outing had been successful.

Coincidentally, when David got back to the dorm he found letters from both Bishop Vander Horst and Jim Coleman about that upcoming relocation to Johnson City. With questions regarding his job description, housing, and the move itself needing answers, logic dictated that as he headed home to Chattanooga it might be a good idea to stop off in the northeast corner of his home state for a day or two to get matters settled.

On Friday, the 7th of May, the Episcureans dined at The Royal Key then went to see *The Andromeda Strain* at the Apex Theater. David, who had seen it already with Patty, felt that the film was good enough to recommend to the group. He also recommended that the four of them get together for one more outing before they all disbanded. That event was scheduled for two weeks later.

On the following Thursday, everyone in the academic community received a letter announcing the resignation of Evelyn Drake as seminary hostess at the end of the year. Her job had been to welcome visitors to the campus, especially those staying in the guest quarters of Moore Hall. Though the Wilmerites had not had all that much direct interaction with her over the years, she represented for them the fact that all they knew and loved at VTS was coming to an end. The Village Inn served a special pitcher of beer that night, as three very close friends toasted one another and gave thanks to God for the time they had shared.

With the end of their seminary career clearly in sight, the members of the 1971 senior class gathered on the following morning in the lobby of Aspinwall Hall for a special service. They used the Order for Celebrating the Holy Eucharist from the authorized book of trial liturgies, on one of the days that had been set aside for experimentation with different styles and types of worship.

As one of the readings for the day, and as had been done in the junior year, a specially prepared epistle was offered, again giving an assessment of how the class perceived itself at that point in time. It was a thoughtful and reflective piece, and although not everyone agreed with everything that was mentioned, still the letter represented well the overall experience of the corporate body.

The composition read as follows:

> As we worship together in the midst of this building, let us pause for a few moments. Let us relax and reflect upon the journey through seminary.
>
> It was right here in this lobby that we began as new seminarians. We entered through that hard-to-open front door . . . and sought security by gazing at these bulletin boards. We felt awkward in this strange place among these even stranger people. And those professors!!! They sure were on top of some very lofty academic pedestals! High and mighty. Threatening . . . we were fearful.
>
> Soon the honeymoon, the dream of going to seminary, was over. Classes, waiter squad, community worship, retreats, grades, little money and many new people flooded in on our lives.
>
> Our first year was a getting-things-straight year. We were going to save the world! All we needed were the proper tools—like Bible . . . preaching . . . theology . . . sensitivity . . . God. We were pretty sure of ourselves. Or were we?
>
> Then clinical training began. Most of us met ourselves for the first extensive time during clinical. 'Fun' isn't exactly the word to describe this experience. 'Interesting' is closer; 'profound,' even closer.
>
> Our middler year was a crusher. We found ourselves fragmented and pressured in seemingly too many directions. We continued to push for the big grade and a pat on the back by a field work supervisor.

We also continued looking at ourselves in colloquy, in ethics, in homiletics. At first we didn't like what we saw—our shortcomings, our sins. We felt judgment and yet . . . we knew there had to be more than this.

As we began to understand our shared predicament—the pressures, the problems, the self-centeredness, the attempts to please others on their terms—we found comfort in the cross of Christ. This cross, this Christ helped us to cope with our predicament by showing us God's willingness to share in our daily dilemmas. We actually got to the point where only half of our class seemed to be out of it. We hoped that eventually they'd come over to our side.

Our sojourn through seminary is concluding with a rapid senior year. This has been a time of love. A time of closeness. A time of new awareness, of confidence and inner strength that we never dreamed was possible. And these gifts have come from beyond us.

Our trip through seminary has been a journey in relationship with God. Where once we felt only judgment, now we know grace. Although our doubts remain, our faith is somehow deeper, nearer our center.

And what of those faculty members? They are dear friends. And what of our classmates? We love each other. And what of our Lord? HE LIVES!! AMEN.

After Dean Woods celebrated Holy Communion, everyone walked over to the steps of Packard-Laird Auditorium for the taking of the class picture. Spouses and children of the married students were already in place, along with at least one family dog. As the seniors sat and posed with peace signs and waves, John and David stood on the back row to hold up a banner that read: "Go Ye Into The World and Preach The Gospel."

That photograph captured the moment, and there was no question that many would cherish it for years to come.

After lunch on Friday the 14th, David departed for his final retreat at Shrinemont with the youth group of St. George's. What he didn't know was that Hedley had flown Patty up and driven her over to the camps and conference center earlier in the day.

When the Tennessean entered the dining hall for supper, he was both surprised and thrilled to find his beloved there to greet him. And that night, instead of what David thought was to be the first session of a weekend agenda, there turned out to be a party given in his honor, as a sign of appreciation for what he had meant to the life of the congregation.

They bestowed on him a crown fashioned out of balloons and gave him numerous gifts to treasure for a lifetime. The presents, along with his girl, accompanied him back to VTS on Sunday. After she left town later that day, David returned to his room in Wilmer Hall with a great sense of thanksgiving—for St. George's and the wonderful parish he had enjoyed being a part of over the past two years, for the wonderful relationship he had shared with Hedley Williams and the parish teens, and certainly for Patty and the time they had been able to spend together during those years.

Later that night, he took pen in hand to write both his family and his girl in order to send them the schedule for graduation activities and to let them know how much he looked forward to seeing them in just a matter of days. Those letters were then mailed with brand new postage stamps, which had just gone up to eight cents apiece.

After a good night's sleep, David took off on the road again. Monday, May 17th, found the Wilmerites departing in Flo for their last class retreat, which was to take place once more at Peterkin Conference Center in Romney, West Virginia. That was the same site where the son of a sports announcer had gotten news of the death of his father. Prayerfully, the time there would not be painful.

Thankfully, it was not. In fact, the forty-eight hours spent in that setting helped to mold the seniors into even more of a cohesive community and family than they had yet to experience. The conversation came easily. The openness was genuine. The sharing touched hearts.

And by the time Wednesday morning arrived for the closing Eucharist, which Chaplain Sanders celebrated, a prayer of thanksgiving had been composed for all of the students present along with a loving description of how they each would be remembered. The list, in no particular order, read as follows:

> **For John Adams** – His athletic prowess, his discovery of himself.
> **For Walt Mycoff** – His gorilla-like walk, a quiet guy with a gigantic heart and mind.
> **For Gary Ramsey** – Our loyal, hard-working representative on various committees.
> **For David Dye** – The mustache and neat black sideburns, his burning desire to heal racial strife.
> **For Burdette Stampley** – The pipe man, the devoted husband who is on a perpetual honeymoon.
> **For David Knight** – The VW lover who walks like a car piston, who is anxious to become a father.
> **For Gary Gillard** – The thinker, structurer of words, God's poet.
> **For Max Nye** – The voice, which sometimes doesn't stop soon enough, caught by and devoted to Christ.

For Bill Deneke – Our beloved convert, a shy guy.

For Don Hanway – The speedy tight end, music lover, scholar.

For Dick Merrill – Of times the joyful heart dancing. Hope he finds work.

For Glenn Busch – Man of the velvet words, the Lord's logician.

For Tom Moore – The baseball slugger, southern gentleman.

For John McDowell – Teacher, tinkerer.

For John Bingham – The big man, smiling, joyful, grace-full.

For Ed Mullins – Financial genius, preacher.

For Don Wimberly – His quiet confidence, affectionate, devout.

For Joe Pennington – The master of the one-liner.

For Clyde Shuler – The psychologist, hard worker.

For Nancy Wicks – Our little lady. Grant her security and comfort.

For Rich Pocalyko – The man who, when his faith hangs by a thread, holds on to his wife, whose faith always hangs by chain link.

For John Lambert – The bearded enthusiast, zesty lover of life.

For Carl Cunningham – His sleepiness, his seriousness, his face breaking into laughter.

For Bob Morrison – The slender man, disciplined, the Virginian.

For Vince Warner – A minister, who cares and really works at living and loving.

For Cliff Pike – Mr. Zip on the football field, carefree, concrete.

For Dick Milner – Frowning, emphatic, incisive, penitent.

For Ken Henry – Our good leader, fast-moving, he combines joy and earnestness into one.

For George Andrews – The most likely to be bishop, creative, devoted family man.

For Bob Redmon – Our plump tenor, a smells and bells man.

For Jim Alby – Our light into the world of the deaf, scholar, a miracle in our midst.

For LaRue Downing – The unpacker of jargon, athlete, friend.

For Peter Winterble – A professional lover of mankind who has got a lot of it all together.

For Jack Isbell – The liturgical innovator, Anglo-Catholic, committed.

For Roy Green – The sophisticated gentleman, sensitive, understanding.

For Bob Kirkpatrick – A great humorist with a passion for life.

For David Chamberlain – The banjo man, who knows suffering and loves because of it.

For John McCann – The man of a thousand gestures, his three-point sermons, his wonderful humor, who won't allow us to take ourselves too seriously.

For Ed Martin – The Rock, the Silver Wolf, the lover of Chris and Rocky, who this year experienced a tremendous sense of grief and sorrow with the loss of a son, who also was the one who said: "And what of our Lord? HE LIVES!!

The last week arrived. On Friday, May 21st, the Episcureans shared their final outing. Dinner took place at the Inn of the Eight Immortals, which specialized in Chinese food.

"David, you're quiet tonight. What's bothering you?" asked his fellow diners.

After taking a moment to collect his thoughts, David replied, "I must tell you, I'm scared to death to be leaving school. We're about to go out into the world as priests, and I still don't have a clue about so many things."

"Like what?" asked John.

"Well, I feel pretty confident as a preacher, but I don't know a thing about parish administration issues. I can't imagine how I'm going to lead a parish when I know absolutely nothing about budget administration, or how to hire and fire employees, or how to operate a mimeograph machine. I can mouth the words that consecrate bread and wine into the body and blood of Christ, but I still don't feel comfortable doing that yet. I still feel unprepared for the road ahead."

With that dam burst, the others joined in—both to air their own fears of the future and to bolster their friends with encouragement that they were not alone in their doubts. After all, somehow those who had gone before them had been able to figure it all out, so surely would they.

Feeling lighter, they drove to the Arlington Theater to view the film called *Mrs. Polifax, Spy*. Back at the dorm after the show, the four friends shared a small bottle of champagne, as a fitting conclusion to the many heartfelt evenings that they had spent together over the past months.

On the following Sunday, David preached his last sermon at St. George's in the context of a folk mass celebrated by Hedley along with the kids. A lovely reception followed, which included the kindest of comments from members of the congregation, a letter of warmest appreciation from the vestry, and a home communion set with pyx (a container for consecrated bread).

But the most meaningful gift, as far as David was concerned, had to be what Hedley told him. The rector divulged that he had called Bishop Jack Vander Horst to see if the Tennessee seminarian might be allowed to stay on and work in the church there. Although the bishop had said no because the senior was needed back in his diocese, the gesture meant everything in the world to the graduate-to-be.

After the festivities concluded David sat in the St. George's parking lot, reflecting for a little while. He read the letter from Cynthia Clark, the register of the vestry, who had been asked to express gratitude for the work he had done, for his enrichment of parish life, for relationships with the young people, for sermons, for meetings attendance, and for acts of friendship. Ms. Clark wished David joy and success, and she expressed the hope that he would come back to visit. David hoped he could, but whatever was to happen, the memories he had of that place would last him a lifetime.

Later in the day, the annual dorm picnic took place back on the hill. There, after the residents enjoyed a flavorsome cookout, one more picture just had to be taken of "The Little Men of Wilmer Hall."

Monday the 24th (John's birthday) followed. Along with other members of his class, he was greeted early that morning with a final report of grades. It was a nice gift for him because the man from Missouri had managed to complete his seminary career with academic honors.

David too was pleased with the overall average of his grades that final quarter, because he had solidified his status as a "B" student. Even with an "A" and two "B's," he was almost amused with the "C" he received in youth ministry because it obviously did not reflect the success with which he had been blessed at St. George's. That fact was better acknowledged with another "S" in field education.

Later that morning, at 11:00 to be exact, there was a graduation rehearsal scheduled, and afterward the dean presented the senior class at the annual alumni luncheon. Then in the afternoon, John celebrated his birthday with a party. Although that was not unusual in and of itself, the event in question just happened to involve the entire class.

Armistead Boothe, affectionately known as "Army," served as a member of the school's administrative staff. One of his claims to fame was his yearly mint julep cocktail party for the graduates. As nice a gesture as that always proved to be, he was mainly remembered for his distinctive julep recipe.

Army's idea of a mint julep seemed to be a glass full of straight bourbon adorned with a sprig of mint. Even so, the drinks were enjoyed, and "a good time was had by all."

On Tuesday, the 25th, family members began to arrive. Bob's mother, John's mother and father, David's mother and grandfather—they all arrived safely at Washington's National Airport to find their "boys" waiting for them to drive them to their reserved hotel rooms in Alexandria. Patty arrived safely as well to stay once more with Mil Ritchie in Arlington. She had driven up from Chattanooga so that she could help her fella transport his possessions back to Tennessee.

The Chamberlain party gathered together that evening for a bite to eat and a quiet celebration. It was hard to believe that the milestone dreamed about for so long had finally arrived. Later, as David turned in for the night, he prayerfully prepared for the beginning of the last act of his life at Virginia Theological Seminary.

CHAPTER 27

Wednesday, May 26th, began with a meeting of the graduates-to-be in order to confirm that all details for the commencement ceremonies were properly in place. Though the middlers were actually in charge of arrangements, each senior acted as a liaison.

Bob was in contact with his successor in charge of academic gowns to make sure everything was in order. John did the same with regard to outdoor activities, as did David with the escorts.

After a last lunch together as a class, individual members were then free to spend the afternoon with family and friends. Bob and John took off with their respective families, while Patty and David treated his mother and grandfather to a tour of Washington. Afterwards, there was enough time left for another bite to eat, as well as an opportunity to freshen up for the evening.

The missionary service, or baccalaureate, began at 8:00 p.m. in the chapel. Voices sang out loudly and clearly with the words of the processional hymn:

> O Word of God incarnate,
> O Wisdom from on high,
> O Truth, unchanged, unchanging,
> O Light of our dark sky;

> We praise thee for the radiance
> That from the hallowed page,
> A lantern to our footsteps,
> Shines on from age to age.

After three more stanzas and opening prayers, the officiant invited the congregation to be seated. Lessons from the Old Testament book of the prophet Isaiah and Paul's New Testament Epistle to the Romans came next. Then, a hymn introduced the reading from Matthew 28:19–20. The very last lines of the evangelist's account included the words known as "The Great Commission." They read:

> Go therefore and make disciples of all nations, baptizing them in the name of the Father and of the Son and of the Holy Spirit, teaching them to observe all that I have commanded you; and lo, I am with you always, to the close of the age.

Another hymn introduced the sermon, which was delivered by the Reverend Robert M. Smith, Rector of Trinity Episcopal Church in Wilmington, Delaware. He elaborated on the text from Matthew in a most unusual way, by relating it to a couple of contemporary songs: "Bridge over Troubled Water" by Simon and Garfunkel, and "I Don't Know How to Love Him" from the musical *Jesus Christ Superstar*. His method of interweaving the message of the gospel with modern culture was most interestingly done and quite effective.

The service then continued with Holy Communion celebrated by Dean Woods. It was an emotional occasion for Bob, David, and John, for it was the final opportunity they would have to go to the altar together. As the three friends knelt at the rail to receive consecrated bread and wine, their prayers were not for themselves, but for one another.

As the members of the congregation began to sing their last hymn of worship for the night, the words of the first stanza reminded them of the faith sustaining them all:

> Let all mortal flesh keep silence,
> And with fear and trembling stand;
> Ponder nothing earthly-minded,
> For with blessing in his hand
> Christ our God to earth descendeth,
> Our full homage to demand.

A splendid reception followed in Scott Lounge. The party was a superb chance for parents and students both to finally meet the ones who meant so much in the lives of the seminarians. David took special pleasure in introducing his mother and grandfather to John, Bob, Jim, Roy, and Carl. Then he motioned Ed over and said to them, "Mom, Granddad, I'd like you to meet Ed Mullins, whom you've heard so much about." The three of them, along with Patty, passed broad smiles and hearty handshakes.

After a good night's sleep, the big day arrived. That morning the campus quadrangle filled with graduates in their academic gowns and hoods as the class of 1971 prepared to graduate from the Protestant Episcopal Theological Seminary in Alexandria, Virginia. On Thursday, May 27th, at 10:30 a.m., the 148th commencement exercise began.

The senior class processed into the chapel to the music of "Purcell's Trumpet Voluntary." With the faculty watching from the chancel, the students took their place in the first few pews of the nave. Fellow Tennessean Carl Cunningham sat with David and also Jim Alby on the front row of the gospel side of the church. John and Don Wimberly, the two class members being awarded the degree of cum laude, sat opposite them on the epistle side with Bob farther down the same row. Roy Green sat just behind Bob.

As the service unfolded, part of St. Paul's letter to the Ephesians began to echo throughout the worship space, especially the seventh verse of the fourth chapter.

"But grace was given to each of us according to the measure of Christ's gift."

Also meaningful were verses eleven and twelve in that same chapter:

"And His gifts were that some should be apostles, some prophets, some evangelists, some pastors and teachers, to equip the saints for the work of ministry, for building up the body of Christ."

As those words were uttered, a good many of the graduates thought about the gifts mentioned in the lesson and whether or not they possessed any of them. Some were quite confident, perhaps too much so, that their talents would prove adequate for the job ahead. Others were not quite so sure that they had the skills needed. But all of the seniors were eager to hear what wisdom would be offered to them in the address that followed the reading.

The Right Reverend Matthew George Henry, Bishop of the Diocese of Western North Carolina and father of class president Ken Henry, stepped up to the microphone. His opening words could not have been better chosen to deflate the egos of some and to comfort those who needed bolstering. Bishop Henry began:

"Senior class, be of good cheer. The church will survive even your ministry."

After nervous laughter trickled through the front pews, silence prevailed, and the speaker knew that he had the attention of his audience. He proceeded to remind his listeners that it was not the job of a clergyman to save the world. Jesus Christ had already accomplished that task. The vocation of a priest was simply to allow that same Lord of life to use the human vessels that He had chosen as channels for His work of reconciling love in the world and to remind all persons of the good news of the gospel, which St. Paul stated so well in Ephesians 2:8–9.

"For by grace you have been saved through faith; and this is not your own doing, it is the gift of God—not because of works, lest any man should boast."

With those thoughts taken to heart, the robed students received degrees as Masters in Divinity and sang hymns. Then—unbelievably—it was over. They had graduated.

Suddenly, the future was upon them. That realization hit the new alumni as they gathered outside the chapel following the service, exchanging greetings, taking pictures, and offering congratulations all around.

Hedley Williams had taken the time to attend the ceremony, and David took special pleasure in introducing the rector of St. George's to his family, right after Patty gave him a big hug. The Episcureans posed for one last picture together, using their fingers to spell out "VTS '71" in sign language.

Around noon, there was a luncheon in the buzzing refectory. Conversation was abundant, hearts were full, spirits were jubilant, and appetites were sated. The only sad thing about the meal was the fact that it would be their final one together in that great hall.

Before everyone departed, Jim Alby gave his classmates a list of ordination dates, as best as he had been able to compile. His own was in Wisconsin on June 10th. Others of note were John McCann in Missouri on June 9th, Ed

Mullins in West Virginia on June 11th, Carl Cunningham in Tennessee on June 27th, Roy Green in Florida on June 29th, and David Chamberlain in Tennessee on July 4th. Bob Redmon's had yet to be determined. Jim added a special request that members of the class make a special point of attending their first reunion in 1976.

Then the farewells began. With the exception of Carl, whom he would see from time to time at diocesan events, David was not sure if or when he would see any of the people in that room again. Of course, some of them he would make a point of getting together with, like Bob and John, but for others, plans were nonexistent.

And what about those faculty members who had meant so much for the past three years, like Molle, Dr. Reid, Dean Woods, and Chaplain Sanders? When would the Tennessean ever lay eyes on them again? It seemed that the majority of his relationships were all dying at the same time—in his field work, at his seminary, with the metropolis of Washington itself, and even with the very books of academic study. Even though all those relationships were ending, the new graduate's faith was firm, and he knew that all would be well because he did indeed believe that death was always followed by resurrection.

After visiting in the dorm with his family for a little while, the future ordinand and his girl drove his family to National Airport for their flight to Chattanooga, then they returned to the holy hill to begin disassembling room #207 in Wilmer Hall.

David and Patty worked on his room for almost two hours before she departed to take Mil Ritchie out to dinner—partly as a way of thanking her for her hospitality on so many different occasions and partly as a way of allowing David one last outing with his comrades. It wound up being a most meaningful evening for each and every one of them.

Bob, David, and John decided to enjoy their last dinner together at one of the first places they had visited in their junior year. Lums was once more the locale for a night of savoring both the food and each other's company.

When the beers arrived, David raised his glass to his compatriots.

"Well, here we are—our last meal together. Someone once said that friends are people who know us well and love us anyway. I would just like to thank you both for loving me anyway."

"Here, here!" grinned Bob and John.

The threesome clinked glasses, then Duck put down his beer.

"I also know, just as that verse in Ephesians Bishop Henry used today says, God loves us regardless of our actions. But it also seems to me that His immeasurable gift of grace has been amplified several times over during our seminary experience. For three years we have been on the same journey together to discover how God reveals Himself to us in our lives and especially in our callings as priests. At this point in the road, we take different forks, but I just want to tell you how much I have loved sharing this road of discovery with you and how grateful I am to God for His priceless gift."

Bob and John returned his sentiments, then they spontaneously began to call out their favorite moments of the past three years. Each Technicolor scene spooled out of their memories like film from a rented projector. Riding in Flo, the Seven-Eleven they only visited once, waiting on refectory tables, playing and singing around the piano in Scott Lounge, the carefree hours of sight-seeing around the nation's capital, their candid conversation beneath the

Washington Monument, nightly prayers and conversations in Wilmer Hall, learning sign language from Jim, Old Testament content quizzes and "Genesis—Once Over Lightly," getting to know the faculty as individuals, the visit to Grace Church in Alexandria, classical music bursting forth from Bob's room, popping corn and watching the Tonight Show, mailing Ember Day letters from that tiny seminary post office, Chuck's Carry-Out and the infamous "unclean" pizza, the camaraderie shared around a table at the local night-time snack spots, watching movies together on a big theater screen, the origin of "the Duck," Dean Trotter's surprise resignation, the flu epidemic, sherry hour, and the parakeet known as "Jigger."

The threesome continued listing their "best of" seminary moments—like ordering their first vestments, the raucous first visit of Bishop Vander Horst, the mellow tones of Peter and Paul and Mary in concert, "The St. Valentine's Day Massacre" skit, the excitement of Patty's visits, Ralph Rat's sojourn from the new Continuing Ed building, the thrill of exploring New York, the satisfaction that came from the work of the Student Aid Society, the introspection of clinical training, exchanging a nightly "blessing," a new beginning with Dean Woods, practicing ministry in their individual field sites, straws drawing liquid from a communal bowl at Trader Vic's, watching as one of their own faculty members become a bishop, capturing seminary life in *Ambo* articles, picking away on an old banjo, delivering their long-anticipated first sermons, John's gentle but firm rule as dorm proctor, the galvanizing Conference on Racism, David's growing film collection, the thunderbolt of losing David's father, the embarrassing thefts in Wilmer Hall, the Fort Hamilton summer, Roy's unexpected marriage to Gail, Ed's mysterious departure from the dorm, the pastoral presence of Chaplain

Sanders, monthly outings of the Episcureans, Upton's locking Price out of his room, celebrating "John McCann Day," the death of John's grandmother, Upton and the jalapeño peppers, the surprise of receiving a master's degree, the great snowball fight, and Army Booth's mint julep recipe.

When at long last they had spent themselves with memories, the discussion naturally turned to the future. John was to head for the Diocese of West Missouri to serve as Curate of Christ Church in Springfield. Bob had decided to stay on in the Northern Virginia area and continue to work at St. Andrew's. David would start in Johnson City the day after his ordination. All three friends were aware of both the excitement and the apprehension that accompanied their plans. Later, as they walked around the quadrangle one final time, the ease of their stride bespoke a shared confidence that their Lord would carry them safely through whatever the church and the world had to offer.

"Don't worry about the future," they had been told so often. "God's already there."

The last morning arrived, a Friday. Patty got to Wilmer Hall early so that she and her fella could finish packing up dorm room #207 and load up the contents into their two automobiles. While she waited in the parking lot, David walked back inside for one remaining box of possessions. As he plodded past Bob's room, his friend poked his head into the hallway.

"Well, Mr. Redmon," David said. "You take care of yourself."

288 A Gift of God

"I love you, man," Bob responded. "You do the same, and include that sweet girl I'm sure you're going to marry. I'll be in touch, and I plan on getting down to see you as soon as I can."

And with that the man from Texas went back inside his room to resume his own packing.

A moment later as David closed his own door for the final time, he paused to listen once more to Mahler's *Eighth Symphony* booming from Bob's record player. At that moment, John walked out of his room with the last of his bags.

"Well, here we are," said the man from Missouri. "It's finally come. I wish that I could really put into words exactly what I feel about the past thirty-three months, but I don't believe that's possible. So, I'll just say what your father said to say—not goodbye, just so long."

The man from Tennessee replied with the only words he felt to be appropriate under the circumstances. Not surprisingly, they were words from a movie—a very special motion picture though, one which they had both seen and shown over and over again.

At the very end of *The High and the Mighty*, Regis Toomey's character utters a line to John Wayne's character as they part company. It was a line that the film collector knew the recipient would appreciate.

"So long," he said. "So long, you ancient pelican."

After walking down the stairs and out the door together, the two of them parted with an exchange of their customary blessing using the sign of the cross, the way they had said good night to one another so many times.

John seated himself behind the wheel of his sky blue Volkswagen, and Duck climbed into "Sam." Having already said her farewells, Patty was waiting in her car to leave when her partner was ready. Bob watched from his window as they all drove away, then with a sigh, he resumed his packing.

John had planned carefully for his two-day trip across country to Missouri, so that he could make the best use of both time and mileage. David, of course, knew his route just as intimately, and with Patty following, he headed west across northern Virginia, later to turn southwest toward Tennessee.

The scenery along interstate highways can be monotonous after a while, but the drive from Front Royal to Roanoke along I-81, which cuts right through the heart of the Shenandoah Valley, escapes that problem by following the highs and lows of the beautiful Blue Ridge Mountains. It was on that road where David Morrow Chamberlain found himself one day, leaving his home to begin a new life in the ministry.

www.ingramcontent.com/pod-product-compliance
Lightning Source LLC
Chambersburg PA
CBHW060005100426
42740CB00010B/1409